U0056847

100% legendary

首選必考
4,000單

「巧取」學測英文15級分+指考英文頂標

洪婉婷◎ 著

學生非讀不可，老師必備的備考聖經！

● **命中率百分百**
收錄學測、指考各年度出現字彙，熟悉反覆出現必考字彙，立即翻轉應試成績。

● **強化記憶連結**
以主題呈現的方式，使大腦能建立較深刻的記憶連結，故事敘述使「必考字彙」烙印在腦海中，串起各必考字彙，建立「點」➡「線」➡「全面」的學習。

● **大幅拓展英文寫作思路**
由卡漫人物敘述掌握英文段落發展，即刻提升英文翻譯能力，並將相關佳句應用於英文寫作，在**學測、指考英文作文**與**翻譯**項目中，獲取佳績。

MP3

Author's
Preface 作者序

完成了「國貿與新多益」及「影響力字彙」之後，想想是時候來點輕鬆有趣的題材了吧。有鑒於媽媽們都很愛看八點檔，女孩兒們都很愛看偶像劇，我開始聯想，有什麼人、事、物是擁有全民魅力，大家都曾幾何時迷到天荒地老的呢？就在這個時候，那個帥帥的蝙蝠俠跟那台令人響往的蝙蝠車突然出現在我的腦海。接踵而來的是超人與他足以推開流星的力量，及美若天仙的神力女超人和那個每個小女生都想要的神奇皇冠與手環！

我曾經幻想，如果我能擁有絕大部分的超能力，那人生不知道會有多麼美好。相信有很多的大朋友小朋友也和我一樣。那就讓我們利用這本書來回想一下英雄們與惡棍們的背景故事，想像一下自己想要成為怎麼樣的英雄人物，同時也輕鬆地增加一些字彙到腦海裡吧。

洪婉婷

Editor's Preface 編者序

在準備學測、指考英文中，許多師生對於準備上仍感到困惑。面對語言科目像是國文、英文，其實在準備上是無範圍的，許多人大概知道要做近十年的考題，但做了歷屆試題且由老師檢討後，知道大概錯在哪了，在實際應考時，卻仍無法於考試中的選擇題拿到滿分。原因在於，每回試題儘管在內容跟難度上的差異，只是檢測當下反應出的成績，並不會於檢討後立即提升寫下回試題或應考的成績。在本身英語閱讀理解、字彙量等綜合能力未提升的同時，寫試題僅僅是了解出題方向，並不會於下次考試中立即提升應考分數。就如同考模擬考時，常會在第一次跟第二次發現自己某個科目仍卡在均標，或是猛 K 後分數卻往下滑。有鑑於此，編輯部規劃了由**卡漫英雄故事**搭配字彙學習的方式，希望讀者拋開課文式的閱讀模式，藉由書中的內容廣泛閱讀，並提升必考字彙量，在應試時即會發現同樣的字只是以不同形式，出現在不同類別的主題裡，可能是單字題、文意選填、篇章結構等等。書中列的字絕對足以應付學測跟指考，最重要的是，別花時間東讀一本、西讀一本，看著桌上的書自亂腳步，從現在起拿起這本並精讀每篇，利用零碎時間聽 MP3 音檔且密集複習，相信其他同學慌慌張張地拿單字卡在背誦時，你內心只覺得更踏實，英語 15 級分根本近在咫尺。　　　　編輯部 敬上

CONTENTS 目次

part1
劃時代的傳奇

學習進度表

Unit 1 Captain America
美國隊長
- ☐ 1-1 成長背景
- ☐ 1-2 超級戰士療程
- ☐ 1-3 圓形盾牌之助
- ☐ 必考字彙大回顧

Unit 2 The Red Skull
紅骷髏
- ☐ 2-1 成長背景
- ☐ 2-2 駭人的紅骷髏
- ☐ 2-3 拯救美國隊長
- ☐ 必考字彙大回顧

Unit 3
Spiderman 蜘蛛人
- ☐ 3-1 成長背景
- ☐ 3-2 覺醒
- ☐ 3-3 感恩節決戰
- ☐ 必考字彙大回顧

Unit 4
The Green Goblin 綠惡魔
- ☐ 4-1 成長背景
- ☐ 4-2 哈利的指責
- ☐ 4-3 惡魔配方
- ☐ 必考字彙大回顧

Unit 5 Batman 蝙蝠俠
- ☐ 5-1 成長背景
- ☐ 5-2 絕佳的能力
- ☐ 5-3 蝙蝠俠的使命
- ☐ 必考字彙大回顧

Unit 6 Joker 小丑
- ☐ 6-1 成長背景
- ☐ 6-2 極端的心理
- ☐ 6-3 化學天才
- ☐ 必考字彙大回顧

Unit 7 Wonder Woman
神力女超人
- ☐ 7-1 成長背景
- ☐ 7-2 神奇的力量
- ☐ 7-3 女性榜樣
- ☐ 必考字彙大回顧

Unit 8 Cheetah 豹女
- ☐ 8-1 成長背景
- ☐ 8-2 眼鏡蛇龍頭捕獲
- ☐ 8-3 嗜血的快感
- ☐ 必考字彙大回顧

Unit 9 Baymax 杯麵
- ☐ 9-1 成長背景
- ☐ 9-2 杯麵的改變
- ☐ 9-3 杯麵的犧牲
- ☐ 必考字彙大回顧

是否能晉升為超能字彙英雄？

★完成10小節 → 「肉雞小英雄」

★完成27小節 → 「小小英雄達人」

★完成36小節 → 「傳奇英雄」

MP3 01

From Nobody to The Chosen One
由默默無聞到雀屏中選

Steve Rogers was born in New York City in the 1920s. As much as he would love to help in World War II, he was **rejected** for the **military recruitments** for **multiple** times due to his **health** and **physical** problems.

Even so, his **enthusiasm** never **dropped**. He again **attempted** to **enlist** during an **exhibition** of future technologies.

Dr. Abraham Erskine **overheard** Roger's **conversation** and decided to put him into the Strategic Scientific Reserve and part of the super-soldier **experiment**.

史蒂夫・羅傑斯出生於1920年代的紐約市。由於他的健康和體格的問題，雖然他很想在二次世界大戰中幫忙，他卻被軍事招聘多次的拒絕。

即便如此，他熱情不懈。他再次在一個未來技術展覽期間嘗試應徵。

亞伯拉罕・厄斯金博士在聽到羅傑的對話後，決定把他送上科學戰略儲備團隊並成為超級戰士實驗的一部分。

In this team, Rogers later on **gained** his **position** as the chosen one with his **intelligence** and **bravery**.

在這個團隊中，羅傑斯後來因為他的智慧與勇氣，成為了雀屏中選的那一位。

卡漫精選字彙表

單字	詞性	中譯	單字	詞性	中譯
health	*n.*	健康	enlist	*v.*	徵募
physical	*adj.*	身體的	exhibition	*n.*	展覽
reject	*v.*	拒絕	overhear	*v.*	無意間聽到
military	*n. / adj.*	軍人/軍隊的	conversation	*n.*	談話
recruitment	*n.*	募兵	experiment	*n.*	實驗
multiple	*adj.*	複合的	gain	*v.*	獲得
enthusiasm	*n.*	熱心，熱忱	position	*n.*	位置
drop	*v.*	中斷	intelligence	*n.*	智慧
attempt	*v.*	企圖	bravery	*n.*	勇敢，勇氣

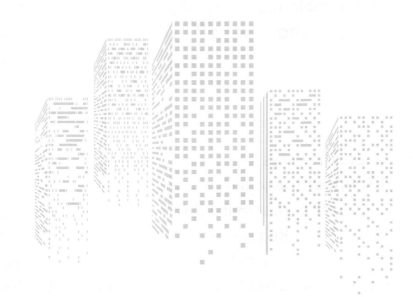

01 劃時代的傳奇

02 不朽的英雄神話

03 無堅不摧背後的英雄血淚

04 永存於人們心中的英雄霸主

Unbeatable Abilities Which Never Wear Out
絕不減弱且不敗的能力

Erskine gave Rogers the super-soldier **treatment**. He was **injected** with a special **serum** and **dosed** with "vita-rays" which made him taller and more **muscular**. From his attributes, such as endurance, agility, durability, and healing power, Rogers has a near superman power. Also with the super-soldier serum **replenished** ability, Rogers abilities do not wear off over time.

Erskine was then killed by one of Schmidt's **assassins**, Heinz Kruger, who later on **committed suicide**. For a long time, Rogers was **touring** the nation in a colorful costume as "Captain America" to **promote** war

厄斯金給了羅傑斯超級戰士的療程。他被注射一種特殊含有「VITA-射線」劑量的血清,這使他的身高和肌肉更為發達。從他的特質,像是耐力、敏捷度、耐久性及自癒能力,羅傑斯有著近超人的能力。另外有著超級戰士血清補給能力,羅傑斯的能力從不會減弱。

厄斯金爾後被施密特的一名刺客亨氏克魯格刺殺身亡,亨氏克魯格後來也自殺了。有很長一段時間,羅傑斯身穿五顏

bonds. During his tour in Italy, Rogers learned that his good friend Barnes might be killed by Schmidt's **forces**.

He **refused** to believe that his friend was dead, and **insisted** to **mount** a solo **rescue**. Rogers **infiltrated** the **fortress** of Schmidt's Hydra organization and freed Barnes and many other prisoners.

六色的「美國隊長」制服在各地販賣戰爭債券。他在義大利旅遊的期間，羅傑斯得知他的好朋友巴恩斯可能被施密特的部隊給殺了。

他拒絕相信他的朋友死了，堅持要安排一個單獨的救援行動。羅傑斯滲透進施密特九頭蛇組織的堡壘，並釋放巴恩斯和許多其他的囚犯。

卡漫精選字彙表

單字	詞性	中譯	單字	詞性	中譯
treatment	n.	治療	commit	v.	犯（罪）
inject	v.	注射	suicide	n.	自殺
serum	n.	血清	tour	n.	旅行，遊覽
dose	n.	一劑	promote	v.	晉升
muscular	adj.	肌肉的	force	v.	強迫
endurance	n.	耐久力	refuse	v.	拒絕
agility	n.	敏捷	insist	v.	堅持
durability	n.	耐久性	mount	v.	登上
healing	n. / adj.	康復	rescue	v.	營救
replenish	v.	補充，備足	infiltrate	v.	滲入
assassin	n.	刺客	fortress	n.	要塞

A Circular Vibranium Shield
圓形振金盾牌

Rogers then was given the **advanced** outfit and equipment, most **notably** a circular shield made of vibranium, a rare, nearly **indestructible** metal. Rogers often uses his shield as an **offensive** throwing weapon. Combining his skills with his shield, he can attack multiple targets in succession with a single throw or even cause a **boomerang**-like return from a throw to attack an enemy from behind.

Rogers and his team later on started an attack to stop Schmidt from using weapons of mass **destruction** on all major cities across the globe. Rogers successfully stopped Schmidt's evil

之後，羅傑斯被賦予了先進的服裝和設備，最值得注意的是用振金所做的圓形盾牌。這是非常難得可見，幾乎堅不可摧的金屬。羅傑斯經常用他的盾牌作為進攻的投擲武器。結合他的技能和他的盾牌，他可以利用單擲連續攻擊多個目標，甚至以迴旋方式從背後攻擊敵人。

羅傑斯和他的團隊後來就開始攻擊在世界各主要城市使用大規模殺傷性武器的施密特。羅傑斯成功阻止了施密特的邪惡

plans, but found that the risk of detonating other weapons made it unlikely for the plane to land, after taking over the plane.

Rogers decided to crash the plane in the Arctic. Everyone thought Rogers was dead. However, Rogers **awakened** in a 1940s-style hospital room nearly 70 years later.

計劃，但卻發現引爆其他武器的風險使得在接手飛機後，飛機無法降落。

羅傑斯決定讓飛機在北極墜毀。大家都以為羅傑斯已經死了。然而，羅傑斯70年後在一個1940年代風格的病房裡醒來了。

卡漫精選字彙表

單字	詞性	中譯	單字	詞性	中譯
advanced	*adj.*	先進的	boomerang	*n.*	回力鏢
notably	*adv.*	顯著地	destruction	*n.*	破壞
indestructible	*adj.*	堅不可摧的	detonate	*v.*	引爆
offensive	*adj.*	冒犯的	awaken	*v.*	覺醒

01 劃時代的傳奇

02 不朽的英雄神話

03 無堅不摧背後的英雄血淚

04 永存於人們心中的英雄霸主

15

必考字彙大回顧

卡漫超給力字彙表

單字	中譯	詞性	反義字	反義字中譯
health	健康	*n.*	illness	疾病
physical	身體的	*adj.*	spiritual	心靈的
reject	拒絕	*v.*	accept	接受
military	軍人/軍隊的	*n. / adj.*	civil	公民的
recruitment	募兵	*n.*	dismissal	解職
multiple	複合的	*adj.*	single	單獨的
enthusiasm	熱心，熱忱	*n.*	apathy	漠不關心
drop	中斷	*v.*	continue	繼續
attempt	企圖	*v.*	neglect	忽略
enlist	徵募	*v.*	discharge	解僱
exhibition	展覽	*n.*		
overhear	無意間聽到	*v.*	ignore	忽視
conversation	談話	*n.*	listening	傾聽
experiment	實驗	*n.*		
gain	獲得	*v.*	lose	失去
position	位置	*n.*	displace	使離開
intelligence	智慧	*n.*	stupidity	愚蠢
bravery	勇敢，勇氣	*n.*	cowardice	膽小
treatment	治療	*n.*	harm	傷害
inject	注射	*v.*	remove	去除
serum	血清	*n.*		
dose	一劑	*n.*		

單字	中譯	詞性	反義字	反義字中譯
muscular	肌肉的	*adj.*	puny	弱小的
endurance	耐久力	*n.*		
agility	敏捷	*n.*	clumsiness	笨拙
durability	耐久性	*n.*	flimsiness	脆弱
healing	康復	*n. / adj.*	hurt	傷害
replenish	補充，備足	*v.*	deplete	用盡
assassin	刺客	*n.*		
commit	犯（罪）	*v.*	abstain	避開
suicide	自殺	*n.*	homicide	殺人
tour	旅行，遊覽	*n.*		
promote	晉升	*v.*	degrade	降級
force	強迫	*v.*	dissuade	勸阻
refuse	拒絕	*v.*	allow	同意
insist	堅持	*v.*	deny	否認
mount	登上	*v.*	descend	下降
rescue	營救	*v.*	harm	傷害
infiltrate	滲入	*v.*		
fortress	要塞	*n.*		
advanced	先進的	*adj.*	behind	落後
notably	顯著地	*adv.*	insignificantly	無足輕重地
indestructible	堅不可摧的	*adj.*	fragile	脆弱的
offensive	冒犯的	*adj.*	inoffensive	無害的
boomerang	回力鏢	*n.*		
destruction	破壞	*n.*	construction	建造
detonate	引爆	*v.*	dismantle	拆下
awaken	覺醒	*v.*	hypnotize	使～催眠

Unit 2
The Red Skull 紅骷髏

2-1　成長背景

The Tragic Childhood
悲慘的童年

Like most **devils**, Johann Schmidt had a **tragic** childhood. Hanging around with the wrong person during his upbringing eventually pushed him to the dark path.

Johann was born in a small village in Germany. His mother died from giving birth to him which drove his **drunken** father to drown the **infant** Johann. Saved by the delivering doctor, Johann's father killed himself, and Johann was **forced** into an **orphanage**.

Johann was having a hard time growing up because he was the kind of kid that was being **bullied**. Johann developed his **anti-social**

如同許多的惡棍，約翰施密特有一個悲慘的童年。成長過程中與錯的人相伴最終將他推向黑暗的道路。

約翰出生在德國的一個小村莊。他的母親在生下他後便死亡，因此他酗酒的父親企圖淹死嬰兒約翰。約翰被接生的醫生救起後，他的父親自殺了。約翰被迫住進一所孤兒院。

約翰的成長過程很辛苦，因為他是被欺負的那種孩子。約翰因此發展了他的反

personality and slowly began to think that every man was his enemy. Johann **eventually** ran away from the orphanage and started his life on the streets.

His first murder killed a **Jewish** girl with a shovel, a girl he liked but rejected him.

社會人格，慢慢開始認為每個人都是他的敵人。約翰最終還是從孤兒院逃離，並開始在大街上生活。

他第一次殺人是用鏟子殺死了一個他喜歡卻拒絕了他的猶太女孩。

卡漫精選字彙表

單字	詞性	中譯	單字	詞性	中譯
devil	*n.*	惡棍	bully	*v.*	欺侮
tragic	*adj.*	悲劇的	anti-social	*adj.*	反社會的
drunken	*adj.*	酗酒的	personality	*n.*	人格
infant	*n.*	嬰兒	eventually	*adv.*	最終，最後
forced	*adj.*	強迫的	jewish	*adj.*	猶太人的
orphanage	*n.*	孤兒院			

MP3 05

The Birth of the Red Skull
紅骷髏的誕生

After years of **shady** work below Hitler, Johann **proudly** became an S.S. Officer. Later on, he was trained **personally** by the Fuhrer of Germany to fit Hitler's requirement, becoming the 2nd most powerful man within Germany. He killed his **former** officer who failed to train him under Hitler's ideals for S.S. Officer. This action **awarded** Johann an officer uniform, rank, and a **trademark** that would be **burnt** into the hearts of those who would **dare oppose** Hitler's **agenda**.

Schmidt's **ambition** to become the **superior** man led him to test the Super Soldier Serum on himself. It didn't go as **smoothly** as Captain America though. Without **proper**

多年來在納粹下做黑幕的工作，約翰自豪地成為S.S.官。後來，他被德國的元首親自培訓，以適應希特勒的要求，成了德國境內第二個最有權勢的人。他殺死了之前沒有成功栽培自己成為希特勒理想S.S官員的前任長官。這個動作使約翰得到了軍官制服、職級，深植在那些想反對希特勒的人心中。

施密特渴望成為超凡的野心導致他將超級戰士的血清測試在自己身上。雖然，他沒有像美國隊長那

treatment and **dosage**, he was **transformed** into the **horrifying** Red Skull. After gaining the **unimaginable** power, he decided to take over the world on his own.

樣的順利。由於沒有適當的治療和劑量，它使他變為駭人的紅骷髏。獲得難以想像的力量後，他決定自己統治世界。

卡漫精選字彙表

單字	詞性	中譯	單字	詞性	中譯
shady	adj.	可疑的，見不得人的	ambition	n.	雄心，報復
proudly	adv.	自負地	superior	adj.	優秀的
personally	adv.	就個人而言	smoothly	adv.	平穩地，順利地
former	adj.	前一任的	proper	adj.	適合的，恰當的
award	v.	授與	dosage	n.	劑量
trademark	n.	商標	transform	v.	改變，轉變
burn	v.	烙印	horrifying	adj.	令人恐懼的
dare	v.	膽敢	unimaginable	adj.	難以想像的
oppose	v.	反對	battle	v.	爭鬥
agenda	n.	日常工作事項			

01 劃時代的傳奇

02 不朽的英雄神話

03 無堅不摧背後的英雄血淚

04 永存於人們心中的英雄霸主

MP3 06

The Last Fight MP3 06
最後一戰

In March 1945, the U.S. Army **attacked** Schmidt's base. **Unfortunately**, Captain America was **captured** by Schmidt's soldiers and was almost killed. In order to **rescue** Rogers, the allied **troops** under Colonel Chester Phillips, Agent Peggy Carter and the Howling Commandos **stormed** the HYDRA **Headquarters** and rescued Rogers.

Rogers and Schmidt started their last fight while Rogers was attempting to **explore** the **cockpit**. Schmidt tried to shoot at Rogers for several times, but was unsuccessful. Instead, Rogers **managed** to throw his shield at Schmidt which not only **knocked** him back but also damaged the

1945年3月，美國軍隊攻擊施密特的基地。不幸的是，美國隊長被施密特的士兵所俘虜，並差點送命。為了搶救羅傑斯，盟軍部隊上校切斯特‧菲利普斯、特使佩吉‧卡特和嚎叫突擊隊衝進HYDRA總部，救出羅傑斯。

當羅傑斯試圖探索駕駛艙時，羅傑斯和施密特開始了他們的最後一戰。施密特試圖射擊羅傑斯好幾次但都沒有成功。相反的，羅傑斯設法用他的盾牌丟向施密特，並成功的使他倒

machine **containing** the Tesseract. Schmidt **accidentally grabbed** the damaged Tesseract which opened a **portal** and **launched** Schmidt into it. Schmidt **vanished** from Earth until years later...

退，但同時也損壞了包含超立方的機器。施密特不小心抓住了受損的超立方。超立方因此打開了一個門戶，並把施密特吸進去。施密特從此從地球上消失了，直到幾年後……

卡漫精選字彙表

單字	詞性	中譯	單字	詞性	中譯
attack	v.	進攻	manage	v.	管理，控制
unfortunately	adv.	不幸地	knock	v.	敲擊
capture	v.	捕獲，俘虜	contain	v.	包含
tescue	v.	救援	accidentally	adv.	意外地
troop	n.	軍隊，部隊	grab	v.	抓
storm	v.	強攻	portal	n.	門戶
headquarter	n.	總部，總公司	launch	v.	發射，發動
explore	v.	探索	vanish	v.	消失
cockpit	n.	駕駛艙			

必考字彙大回顧

卡漫超給力字彙表

單字	中譯	詞性	反義字	反義字中譯
devil	惡棍	*n.*	angle	天使
tragic	悲劇的	*adj.*	comic	喜劇的
drunken	酗酒的	*adj.*	sober	不過量飲酒的
infant	嬰兒	*n.*	adult	成年人
forced	強迫的	*adj.*	voluntarily	自願地
orphanage	孤兒院	*n.*		
bully	欺侮	*v.*	please	討好
anti-social	反社會的	*adj.*	social	社交的
personality	人格	*n.*		
eventually	最終，最後	*adv.*	immediately	立即
jewish	猶太人的	*adj.*		
shady	可疑的，見不得人的	*adj.*	honest	老實的
proudly	自負地	*adv.*	humbly	謙遜地
personally	就個人而言	*adv.*	generally	廣泛地
former	前一任的	*adj.*	current	現任的
award	授與	*v.*	withhold	不給，抑制
trademark	商標	*n.*		
burn	烙印	*v.*	extinguish	平息
dare	膽敢	*v.*	abstain	避免
oppose	反對	*v.*	agree	同意
agenda	日常工作事項	*n.*		

單字	中譯	詞性	反義字	反義字中譯
ambition	雄心，報復	*n.*	apathy	冷淡
superior	優秀的	*adj.*	ordinary	平凡的
smoothly	平穩地，順利地	*adv.*	difficultly	困難地
proper	適合的，恰當的	*adj.*	inappropriate	不適當的
dosage	劑量	*n.*		
transform	改變，轉變	*v.*	remain	維持
horrifying	令人恐懼的	*adj.*	delightful	令人愉快的
unimaginable	難以想像的	*adj.*	conceivable	可想像的
battle	爭鬥	*v.*		
firm	穩固的	*adj.*	unstable	不穩的
attack	進攻	*v.*	defend	防禦
unfortunately	不幸地	*adv.*	luckily	幸運地
capture	捕獲，俘虜	*v.*	release	釋放
rescue	救援	*v.*	abandon	拋棄
troop	軍隊，部隊	*n.*	individual	個人
storm	強攻	*v.*	sew	縫合
headquarter	總部，總公司	*n.*		
explore	探索	*v.*	neglect	忽視
cockpit	駕駛艙	*n.*		
manage	管理，控制	*v.*	mismanage	失當處理
knock	敲擊	*v.*		
contain	包含	*v.*	exclude	不包含
accidentally	意外地	*adv.*	on purpose	故意的
grab	抓	*v.*	liberate	解放
portal	門戶	*n.*		
launch	發射，發動	*v.*	receive	接收
vanish	消失	*v.*	appear	出現

01 劃時代的傳奇

02 不朽的英雄神話

03 無堅不摧背後的英雄血淚

04 永存於人們心中的英雄霸主

25

Bitten by A Radioactive Spider
被放射性蜘蛛咬傷

Both his parents were killed in a plane crash, so Peter Parker was raised by his Uncle Ben and Aunt May in Forest Hills, Queens, New York. During his high school years, even though he was known as a science-**whiz**, he was extremely shy and was targeted by his peers.

When he was 15 years old, he attended a public science exhibition and was bitten on the hand by a **radioactive** spider. Instead of getting ill from the **poison**, Parker **magically** gained the ability to **adhere** to walls and ceilings. He also **acquired** the **agility** and **proportionate** strength just like a spider. As a science genius, he

父母都在一次飛機失事中喪生，所以彼得‧帕克是由他的班叔叔及梅阿姨在皇后區的森林山所扶養長大。在他高中時，儘管他被公認為一個科學奇才，他非常害羞，並且是同儕欺侮的目標。

在他15歲時，他參加了一個公開的科學展覽，並被放射性的蜘蛛咬傷了手。非但沒有因為毒藥而生病，帕克神奇獲得了爬牆壁和天花板的能力。他還獲得了敏捷性和相稱性，就跟一隻蜘蛛一樣。作為一

then developed a **gadget** that allows him to fire **adhesive** webbing through wrist-mounted barrels.

門科學天才，他隨後開發出一個小工具，讓他可以藉由腕帶式的機具發射有黏性的蜘蛛網。

As a shy boy, as much as he wanted to **capitalize** on his new abilities, he was too afraid to use his own identity. Therefore, he developed the Spider-Man costume and became a **novel** TV star.

作為一個害羞的少年，雖然他希望可以利用他新的能力，但他非常害怕使用自己的身份。因此，他開發出了蜘蛛人的服裝，並成為一個新奇的電視明星。

卡漫精選字彙表

單字	詞性	中譯	單字	詞性	中譯
radioactive	*adj.*	放射性的	acquire	*v.*	取得，獲得
whiz	*n.*	奇才	agility	*n.*	敏捷
extremely	*adv.*	極端地	proportionate	*v.*	使相稱
peer	*n.*	同輩	gadget	*n.*	器具
poison	*n.*	毒藥	adhesive	*adj.*	有黏性的
magically	*adv.*	不可思議地	capitalize	*v.*	利用
adhere	*v.*	遵守	novel	*adj.*	新穎的

01 劃時代的傳奇

02 不朽的英雄神話

03 無堅不摧背後的英雄血淚

04 永存於人們心中的英雄霸主

With Great Power There Must Also Come – Great Responsibility
強大力量後跟隨而來的是 － 重大的責任

Different from other Superheroes like Batman or Superman who are handsome or rich, Spider-Man lived with his aunt May in a tiny apartment in New York and was **struggling** to make a living, even to pay the rent.

Due to his lonely and **bullied** teenage life, Parker got used to ignoring any **incidents** that happened close to him. Because of that, he missed the chance to stop a **fleeing** thief who robbed and killed his dearly beloved uncle Ben.

Parker **regretted** that he didn't pay enough attention to his surroundings and society. Then,

與蝙蝠俠、超人等可能帥氣或富有的其他超級英雄不同，蜘蛛人與他的阿姨住在紐約的一個小公寓，努力謀生，甚至連交房租都很掙扎。

由於他孤獨且被欺負的青少年生活，帕克習慣性的忽略任何發生在他身邊的事件。正因為如此，他錯過了可以阻止搶劫並殺害他最親愛班叔叔的小偷的機會。

帕克對於自己不夠重視周圍環境及社會這件事感到遺憾。

the principle which his uncle had taught him - "With great power there must also come – great responsibility!" was a huge awakening to him.

於是，他叔叔教他的原則－「強大力量後跟隨而來的是一重大的責任！」使他有很大的覺醒。

卡漫精選字彙表

單字	詞性	中譯	單字	詞性	中譯
struggle	*v.*	掙扎	flee	*v.*	逃走
bully	*v.*	脅迫；欺侮	regret	*v.*	懊悔
incident	*n.*	事件			

01 劃時代的傳奇

02 不朽的英雄神話

03 無堅不摧背後的英雄血淚

04 永存於人們心中的英雄霸主

Best Friend, Girlfriend and the Enemies
摯友，女友及敵人

He **enrolled** at Empire State University after high school where he met his best friend Harry Osborn and his girlfriend Gwen Stacy. The tragedy started there. Gwen's father, George Stacy, an NYPD police officer was accidentally killed during a fight between Spider-Man and Doctor Octopus. Gwen **blamed** Spider-Man for the death for years but **eventually** forgave him.

Harry Osborn's father, Norman Osborn, was the founder of Oscorp, an organization known for supplying weapons to the military. Once during the United States Army visit, Norman **exposed** himself to a new super soldier formula

高中畢業後，他就讀於帝國州立大學，並認識了他最好的朋友哈利・奧斯本和他的女友格溫・史黛西。這正是悲劇的開始。格溫的父親，喬治・史黛西，一個紐約市的警察在蜘蛛人和章魚博士鬥爭之中不幸喪生。格溫多年來指責蜘蛛人，但最終還是原諒了他。

哈利・奧斯本的父親，諾曼・奧斯本，是Oscorp的創始人。Oscorp是著名的軍事武器供應商。一次在美國軍隊走訪時，諾曼讓自己

which was still **unstable**. He gained superhuman strength but went **insane** as well. He then became one of Spider-Man's biggest enemies, the Green Goblin.

During a Thanksgiving fight between the Green Goblin and Spider-Man, Norman accidentally found out that Spider-Man was indeed Peter Parker. Unable to partner with Spider-Man and gain the most **benefits,** Norman kidnapped Gwen and threw her off from a tower of the Brooklyn Bridge, marking a tragic end.

嘗試了一個新的超級戰士配方，雖然這個配方仍不穩定。他獲得了超人的力量，但同時也瘋了。隨後他成為蜘蛛人最大的敵人之一，綠惡魔。

在綠惡魔和蜘蛛人之間的感恩節鬥爭中，諾曼無意中發現了蜘蛛人其實是彼得·帕克。無法與蜘蛛人成為合作夥伴並獲得最大的利益，諾曼綁架了格溫，並從布魯克林大橋的塔上將她扔下，標誌著悲慘的結局。

01 劃時代的傳奇

02 不朽的英雄神話

03 無堅不摧背後的英雄血淚

04 永存於人們心中的英雄霸主

卡漫精選字彙表

單字	詞性	中譯	單字	詞性	中譯
enroll	*v.*	登記	unstable	*adj.*	不穩固的
blame	*v.*	責備，指責	insane	*adj.*	瘋狂的
eventually	*adv.*	最後，終於	benefit	*n.*	好處；優勢
expose	*v.*	使暴露於			

必考字彙大回顧

卡漫超給力字彙表

單字	中譯	詞性	反義字	反義字中譯
radioactive	放射性的	*adj.*		
whiz	奇才	*n.*	amateur	外行的人
extremely	極端地	*adv.*	somewhat	稍微
peer	同輩	*n.*		
poison	毒藥	*n.*	antidote	解藥
magically	不可思議地	*adv.*		
adhere	遵守	*v.*	abandon	放棄
acquire	取得，獲得	*v.*	lose	失去
agility	敏捷	*n.*	stiffness	僵硬
proportionate	使相稱	*v.*	disproportionate	不成比例
gadget	器具	*n.*		
adhesive	有黏性的	*adj.*	unattachable	不黏的
capitalize	利用	*v.*	forfeit	喪失
novelty	新穎	*n.*	stagnation	停滯
bully	脅迫；欺侮	*v.*	please	討好
incident	事件	*n.*		
flee	逃走	*v.*	face	面對
regret	懊悔	*v.*	approve	批准
struggle	掙扎	*v.*	rest	休息
enroll	登記	*v.*	decline	婉拒
blame	責備，指責	*v.*	compliment	讚揚

單字	中譯	詞性	反義字	反義字中譯
eventually	最後，終於	*adv.*	**immediately**	立即
expose	使暴露於	*v.*	**cover**	覆蓋
unstable	不穩固的	*adj.*	**steady**	穩定的
insane	瘋狂的	*adj.*	**sane**	明智的
benefit	好處；優勢	*n.*	**disadvantage**	壞處

MP3 10

The Tragic Early Life Develops the Ambition
早期的悲哀生活所帶來的野心

Born and raised in New Haven, Connecticut, Norman was **abused** by his **alcoholic** father, Amberson Osborn, when he was a child. Norman met his wife in college while he was studying chemistry and electrical engineering. Unfortunately, Norman's wife died soon after having Harry due to illness. Norman needed the job to shift his **focus** that he lost his wife which resulted in **neglect** to his son Harry.

出生並成長於康乃狄克州,諾曼小時候便被他酗酒的父親,安倍森‧奧斯本所虐待。諾曼在大學讀化學和電氣工程時認識了他的妻子,不幸的是,諾曼的妻子在有了哈利不久後,因病去世。諾曼必須專注於自己的工作,才能忘記失去妻子的痛苦,因而在情感上忽略哈利。

Although Norman already was the president of Oscorp, he was not satisfied with his power within the company. His ambition led him to **accuse** Stromm of **embezzlement** and had Stromm **arrested**.

雖然,諾曼已是Oscorp的老闆,但他對於所擁有公司內部的權力並不滿足。他的野心使他指責史湯姆貪污並使史湯姆

被逮捕。

After gaining the full power to control Oscorp, Norman once discovered that Stromm had developed a strength and **intelligence enhancement** formula, but it was still **experimental**. Norman did not care. He attempted to create the formula, but the formula turned green and exploded in his face. The formula indeed increased his intelligence and strength, but the side effect was that it led him to **destructive** insanity.

在獲得Oscorp的完全掌控權後，諾曼有一次發現史湯姆開發了一種可以提升力量及智慧的配方，雖然這個配方仍是實驗性的。諾曼並不在意。他試圖創造這個配方，但配方變為了綠色，並在他的臉上爆炸。這個配方確實增加了他的智慧和力量，但副作用是它導致了他精神錯亂。

卡漫精選字彙表

單字	詞性	中譯	單字	詞性	中譯
ambition	*n.*	雄心，抱負	embezzlement	*n.*	盜用公款
abuse	*n.*	虐待；傷害	arrest	*v.*	逮捕
alcoholic	*n.*	酒鬼	intelligence	*n.*	智慧
focus	*v.*	專注於	enhancement	*n.*	提高，增加
emotionally	*adj.*	感情上；情緒上	experimental	*adj.*	實驗性的
neglect	*v.*	忽視，忽略	destructive	*adj.*	毀滅性的
accuse	*v.*	指控，控告			

01 劃時代的傳奇

02 不朽的英雄神話

03 無堅不摧背後的英雄血淚

04 永存於人們心中的英雄霸主

MP3 11

The Birth and Death of the Green Goblin
綠惡魔的誕生與死亡

Norman Osborn then created his secret identity as the Green Goblin. What he did was become the boss who organizes all the crimes in the city. His desire to **enlarge** his business and the insanity he got from the formula led him down the road of no return. Norman first **intended** to **cement** his position by having a **partnership** with Spider-Man, but it was unsuccessful. He then held a great **grudge** against Spider-Man.

Eventually, he found out that Spider-Man was his son's best friend, Peter Parker. In order to get back at Spider-Man for **refusing** to work with him, the Green Goblin **kidnapped** Parker's girlfriend, Gwen Stacy, and pushed her off the

諾曼・奧斯本爾後創造了他的秘密身份—綠惡魔。他組織全市的罪犯,並成為他們的主腦。他的目的是擴大他的事業。而他從配方所得到的精神錯亂導致他的不歸路。諾曼本想利用與蜘蛛人合作來鞏固他的地位,但並不成功。他因此非常怨恨蜘蛛人。

最終,他發現了蜘蛛人是他兒子最好的朋友,彼得・帕克。為了報復蜘蛛人拒絕與他合作,綠惡魔綁架了帕克的女友格溫・史黛西,並把

Brooklyn Bridge. Spider-Man couldn't help but go for revenge.

During the ensuing battle, Norman was **impaled** by his own goblin glider. He was pronounced dead. Spider-Man took Norman's body back to his penthouse apartment. While Parker was placing his body on the sofa, Harry saw them and **thusly** blamed Parker for Norman's death.

她丟下布魯克林大橋。蜘蛛人忍無可忍決定報復。

在隨後的戰鬥中，諾曼被他自己的惡魔滑翔機刺穿。他被判定死亡。蜘蛛人帶著諾曼的屍體回到他的複合式公寓。當帕克將他的屍體安放在沙發上時，哈利看到了他們，正是如此，哈利將諾曼的死歸咎給帕克。

卡漫精選字彙表

單字	詞性	中譯	單字	詞性	中譯
enlarge	*v.*	擴大	refuse	*v.*	拒絕
intend	*v.*	打算	kidnap	*v.*	綁架
cement	*v.*	鞏固，加強	impale	*v.*	刺穿
partnership	*n.*	合夥	thusly	*adv.*	因此
grudge	*n.*	怨恨			

01 劃時代的傳奇

02 不朽的英雄神話

03 無堅不摧背後的英雄血淚

04 永存於人們心中的英雄霸主

Reborn and Revenge
重生與復仇

While at the **morgue**, the goblin formula's healing factor restored Norman's life. He escaped from the morgue and went to Europe. Since he was believed dead by the general public, he started his evil revenge plans to get back at Spider-Man. His most **significant** work was to **utilize** his fortune to build a **vast** network of criminals to help engineer the nearly impossibly complex and **meticulously** planned plot to destroy Spider-Man.

Although Norman seemed to be **indestructible** after turning into the Green Goblin, his personality was strongly **augmented** by the serum. He suffered from **manic** depression, anti-social **psychopathic**

在太平間時，諾曼被惡魔配方所修復並重生。他從太平間逃出，並去了歐洲。因為普羅大眾認為諾曼已死，他開始了回去報復蜘蛛人的邪惡復仇計劃。他最厲害的工作是利用他的財富建造犯罪分子的網絡，以幫助工程師設計超乎複雜、精心策劃的蜘蛛人復仇計畫。

雖然諾曼成為了堅不可摧的綠惡魔，但他的個性被血清強烈的影響，而受躁狂抑鬱症、到反社會精神病多重人格障礙

traits, and multi-personality **disorder**.

Norman was also highly **sadistic**, showing a complete lack of **empathy** for the lives of innocent people who stand between him and his objectives. It is fair to say that even though Norman thought he owned the power to rule the world, he was not capable of handling himself.

等。

諾曼也非常殘暴，對於站在他和他的目標之間的無辜生命，完全缺乏同情。可以說，即使諾曼認為他擁有統治世界的力量，他卻沒有能力處理自己。

卡漫精選字彙表

單字	詞性	中譯	單字	詞性	中譯
morgue	*n.*	陳屍所	manic	*adj.*	躁狂的
significant	*adj.*	重大的	psychopathic	*adj.*	精神病的
utilize	*v.*	利用	trait	*n.*	特徵
vast	*adj.*	巨大的	disorder	*n.*	失調
meticulously	*adv.*	一絲不苟地	sadistic	*adj.*	殘酷成性的
indestructible	*adj.*	不滅的	empathy	*n.*	同感
augment	*v.*	加強；提高			

必考字彙大回顧

卡漫超給力字彙表

單字	中譯	詞性	反義字	反義字中譯
ambition	雄心，抱負	*n.*	apathy	冷淡
abuse	虐待；傷害	*n.*	look after	照顧
alcoholic	酒鬼	*n.*	teetotaler	滴酒不沾
focus	專注於	*v.*	ignore	忽視
emotionally	感情上；情緒上	*adj.*	objectively	客觀的
neglect	忽視，忽略	*v.*	attempt	嘗試
accuse	指控，控告	*v.*	defend	保衛
embezzlement	盜用公款	*n.*		
arrest	逮捕	*v.*	release	釋放
intelligence	智慧	*n.*	stupidity	愚笨
enhancement	提高，增加	*n.*	Reduce	降低
experimental	實驗性的	*adj.*	tested	測試過的
destructive	毀滅性的	*adj.*	constructive	建設性的
enlarge	擴大	*v.*	shrink	收縮
intend	打算	*v.*		
cement	鞏固，加強	*v.*	detach	分離
partnership	合夥	*n.*	separation	分割
grudge	怨恨	*n.*	friendliness	友好
refuse	拒絕	*v.*	accept	接受
kidnap	綁架	*v.*	free	自由

單字	中譯	詞性	反義字	反義字中譯
impale	刺穿	*v.*		
thusly	因此	*adv.*		
morgue	陳屍所	*n.*		
significant	重大的	*adj.*	minor	次要的
utilize	利用	*v.*	cease	終止
vast	巨大的	*adj.*	miniature	微型的
meticulously	一絲不苟地	*adv.*	inadequately	充分地
indestructible	不滅的	*adj.*	perishable	易腐爛的
augment	加強；提高	*v.*	diminish	減少
manic	躁狂的	*adj.*	calm	冷靜的
psychopathic	精神病的	*adj.*		
trait	特徵	*n.*		
disorder	失調	*n.*	order	順序
sadistic	殘酷成性的	*adj.*	humane	人道的
empathy	同感	*n.*	disagree	不同意

01 劃時代的傳奇

02 不朽的英雄神話

03 無堅不摧背後的英雄血淚

04 永存於人們心中的英雄霸主

MP3 13

Traumatized but Swore Revenge
受到創傷，但誓言復仇

Bruce Wayne was born into a wealthy family in Gotham City. When he was a kid, he witnessed his parents, the **physician** Dr. Thomas Wayne and his wife Martha Wayne, getting murdered by a **mugger** with a gun in front of his very eyes.

He was traumatized but swore revenge in all criminals. Growing up, he became a successful business **magnate**. He was an American billionaire and owned the Wayne Enterprises. In his everyday identity, he acted like a playboy, a heavy drinker, just like many other wealthy men.

布魯斯・韋恩出生在高譚市一個富裕的家庭。當他還是個孩子時，他眼睜睜的看著他的父母，托馬斯・韋恩博士和他的妻子瑪莎・韋恩，被一個搶劫犯槍殺身亡。

他受到創傷，但誓言對罪犯復仇。長大後，他成為了一個成功的商業鉅子。他是美國的一個億萬富翁，並擁有韋恩企業。他日常的身份，就像一個花花公子，天天喝酒，就與許多其他有錢的男人一樣。

But in reality, he did his best **maintaining** his physical **fitness** and mental **acuity**.

He also developed a bat inspired **persona** to fight crime. Dressing up as Batman, Wayne kept the city safe and fought against crimes for most of his night life.

但在現實中，他保持最好的體能和敏銳的智能。

他也開發了一個由蝙蝠作為啟發的人物來打擊犯罪。裝扮成蝙蝠俠，韋恩在他大部分的夜生活時保持城市的安全及打擊犯罪。

卡漫精選字彙表

單字	詞性	中譯	單字	詞性	中譯
traumatize	*v.*	使受精神創傷	maintain	*v.*	維持；保持
physician	*n.*	醫師	fitness	*n.*	健康
mugger	*n.*	強盜	persona	*n.*	角色
magnate	*n.*	巨頭			

Superhero Without Superpower
沒有超能力的超級英雄

Batman does not **possess** any superpowers.

He relies on his genius intellect, physical **prowess**, martial arts abilities, **detective** skills, science and technology, vast wealth, and an **indomitable** will.

Even Superman considers Batman to be one of the most brilliant human beings on the planet.

One of the reasons why he trains himself to become one of the best fighters is that he **refuses** to use guns during battles since it is the weapon that killed his parents.

蝙蝠俠沒有任何超能力。

他依靠他天生的智慧、高強的體能、精湛的武藝、偵探的技能、科學與技術、巨大的財富和不屈不撓的意志。

即便是超人都認為蝙蝠俠是這個星球上最聰明的人類之一。

他將自己訓練成為最好的戰鬥武器之一的原因，是因為他在戰鬥過程中拒絕使用的槍枝，因為它是

He travels around the world to acquire the skills needed to bring criminals to justice.

殺害其父母的武器。

他周遊世界各地取得技能，讓他可以將罪犯繩之以法。

卡漫精選字彙表

單字	詞性	中譯	單字	詞性	中譯
possess	*v.*	具有；佔有	indomitable	*adj.*	不氣餒的
prowess	*n.*	英勇；無畏	refuse	*v.*	拒絕
detective	*adj.*	偵探的			

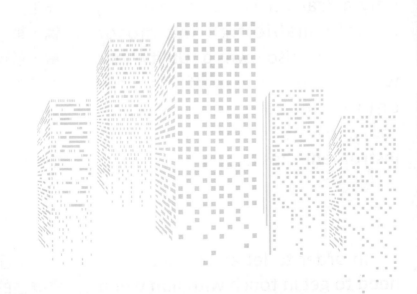

Top Gadgets and Support Go a Long Way
最好的工具和盟友可以走很長的路

Besides mental and physical training, Wayne's **inexhaustible** wealth allows him access to the greatest and most advanced technology, furthermore building the overall top gadgets.

Starting with Batmobile, the **primary** vehicle of Batman, it is not only a "car". It is a self-powered, transformable fighting motor vehicle. He also owns a "**Utility** belt" which keeps most of his field equipment, the crime-fighting tools, weapons, and **investigative** instruments besides guns.

In order to let all the people in need to get in touch with him when

除了心理和體能訓練之外，韋恩取之不盡、用之不竭的財富讓他可以利用最好，也最先進的科技來構建最好的工具。

從蝙蝠車開始，這是蝙蝠俠的主要交通工具。它不僅是一輛「車」，它自發供電，並可轉換成戰鬥摩托車。他還擁有一個「功能腰帶」，這個腰帶裡放置了他大部分在打擊犯罪的工具、武器和調查儀器，除了槍枝以外。

並且為了讓所有需要他的人能與他取

needed, he also set up a whole bunch of Bat-Signals on top of buildings.

When he sees the bat symbol from anywhere in Gotham City, he knows his mission is on. He also gets supports from his **butler** Alfred, **commissioner** Jim Gordon, and **vigilante** allies such as Robin.

得聯繫，他還在建築物頂端設立了一大堆蝙蝠信號。

當他在任何地方看到在高譚市裡的蝙蝠象徵，他便知道那是他的使命。他也從他的管家阿爾弗雷德，專員戈登‧吉姆和維持治安的盟友，如羅賓那裡得到支持。

卡漫精選字彙表

單字	詞性	中譯	單字	詞性	中譯
inexhaustible	*adj.*	無窮無盡的	butler	*n.*	男管家
primary	*adj.*	初級的	commissioner	*n.*	長官
utility	*n.*	公用事業	vigilante	*n.*	正義使者
investigative	*adj.*	調查的			

01 劃時代的傳奇

02 不朽的英雄神話

03 無堅不摧背後的英雄血淚

04 永存於人們心中的英雄霸主

必考字彙大回顧

卡漫超給力字彙表

單字	中譯	詞性	反義字	反義字中譯
traumatize	使受精神創傷	*v.*	soothe	使平靜
physician	醫師	*n.*		
mugger	強盜	*n.*		
magnate	巨頭	*n.*	nobody	小人物
maintain	維持；保持	*v.*	destroy	破壞
fitness	健康	*n.*	weakness	軟弱
persona	角色	*n.*		
possess	具有；佔有	*v.*	lack	缺乏
prowess	英勇；無畏	*n.*	cowardice	怯懦
detective	偵探的	*adj.*		
indomitable	不氣餒的	*adj.*	submissive	服從的
refuse	拒絕	*v.*	accept	接受
inexhaustible	無窮無盡的	*adj.*	limited	有限的
primary	初級的	*adj.*	advanced	高級的
utility	公用事業	*n.*		
investigative	調查的	*adj.*		
butler	男管家	*n.*	master	主人
commissioner	長官	*n.*		
vigilante	正義使者	*n.*		

Unit 6
The Joker 小丑

6-1　成長背景

 The Bleached White Skin, Red Lips and Green Hair
漂到白皙的皮膚，紅潤的嘴唇和綠色的頭髮

No one really knows where this bleached white skin, red lips, and green hair joker actually came from. There is one **indication** that says that the Joker quitted his job to become a stand-up **comedian** to support his wife. Economic conditions led to his agreement with a **robbery**. Although the robbery was successful, the Joker fell into a giant chemical vat when he attempted to **escape** from Batman. The chemical inside the vat changed the whole look of Joker. Even worse, the Joker found out that both his wife and unborn child were dead due to an accident.

沒有人真正知道這個皮膚漂到白皙、紅潤的嘴唇、綠色的頭髮的小丑實際上是從哪裡來的。有一個說法是，小丑辭去了工作，成為一個丑角來支持他的妻子。但實際上沒有那麼順利，經濟狀況使他同意了幫忙搶劫。搶劫雖然成功，但小丑在他試圖從蝙蝠俠那裡逃脫時，掉進了一個化學大桶。甕內的化學藥劑改變小丑的整個外觀。更糟的是，小丑發現，他的妻子和未出生的孩子在一場意外中身亡。

The Joker went insane and became the evil Joker that we know today. He also put the blame on Batman because he believes that had it not been for Batman, he would not have become **disfigured** and his family wouldn't have died. It was all Batman's fault!

小丑瘋了，成了我們今天知道的邪惡的小丑。他也把責任推給蝙蝠俠，因為他認為，如果不是因為蝙蝠俠，他不會毀容，他的家人也不會死。這全都是蝙蝠俠的錯！

卡漫精選字彙表

單字	詞性	中譯	單字	詞性	中譯
bleach	v.	漂白	robbery	n.	搶劫
indication	n.	指示	escape	v.	逃脫
comedian	n.	諧星	disfigure	v.	使……難看

Spectacle is More Important Than Success
場面比成功更重要

The Joker is obsessed with Batman. Every crime The Joker does is to get Batman's attention. From murder, theft to **terrorism**, nothing scares the man in the purple suite with a long-tailed jacket, the string tie, the striped pants, and the pointed-toe shoes. He once claimed that he had killed more than 2000 people. Joker is an **extreme psychopath** that thinks everything he does is funny and humorous. However, they are only funny to himself. Of course The Joker had been caught by the police and sent to justice, but he was always found not guilty by reason of insanity and sent to Arkham Asylum instead of getting the death **penalty.**

小丑纏住了蝙蝠俠。每個小丑所犯的罪，都是要得到蝙蝠俠的關注。從謀殺，盜竊，到恐怖主義，沒有一件是長尾外套、紫色西裝、條紋領帶、條紋褲、尖頭鞋的男人所害怕的。他曾經聲稱，他殺害了2000餘人。小丑是一個極端的心理變態，並認為他所做的一切是有趣和幽默的。然而，只有他一人覺得好笑。當然，小丑也曾經被警察抓，並送到矯正署，但他始終沒有被判重罪。他因為精神錯亂而無罪，並被送往瘋

The Joker **repeatedly** challenges Batman, trying to prove to the world that if the most **orderly** and self-controlling human being as Batman can murder, then anyone is **capable** of becoming a monster like him. To Joker, "**Spectacle**" is more important than success. Therefore, he enjoys making a scene when he commits a crime. To him, if it is not spectacular, it is boring.

人院，而不是死刑。

小丑一再挑戰蝙蝠俠，因為他正試圖向世界證明，如果最有秩序和自我控制的蝙蝠俠都會殺人，那麼任何人都能夠成為像他那樣的怪物。對小丑來說「場面」是比成功更重要的。因此，當他犯罪時，他喜歡大吵大鬧。在他看來，如果不壯觀，則很無聊。

01 劃時代的傳奇

02 不朽的英雄神話

03 無堅不摧背後的英雄血淚

04 永存於人們心中的英雄霸主

卡漫精選字彙表

單字	詞性	中譯	單字	詞性	中譯
terrorism	*n.*	恐怖行動	repeatedly	*adv.*	不停地
extreme	*adj.*	極度的	orderly	*adj.*	有條理的
psychopath	*n.*	精神病患者	capable	*adj.*	有……能力的
penalty	*n.*	懲罰	spectacle	*n.*	公開

The Total Opposite
完全相反

The Joker is crazy but intelligent. He has no superhuman abilities, but he uses his chemical genius to create his most **notable** weapons, such as Jack-in-the boxes with **unpleasant** surprises, and the Joker **venom** which sends its targets into fits of **uncontrollable** laughter and eventually leads to **paralysis**, **coma** or death.

The scariest thing is that the Joker does not own a chemistry factory or lab. With his intelligence, he can manufacture the toxin from ordinary household chemicals and he is the only one that knows the formula.

People describe Batman and

小丑是個瘋子，但很聰明。他沒有超人的能力，但他利用他化學的天才，創造他最著名的武器，如令人不愉快的意外箱，或可以使目標陷入無法控制前俯後仰的狂笑，最終導致癱瘓、昏迷或死亡的小丑毒液。

最可怕的是，小丑並不擁有化學工廠或實驗室。他利用他的智慧，從普通的日用化工材料創造出毒藥，而且他是唯一一個知道公式的人。

人們形容蝙蝠俠

The Joker the two total opposite as the yin and yang. In most stories, the hero normally represents "**Brightness**" and the villain represents "Darkness." However, in Batman and Joker's case, it is the opposite. Batman is the one that lives in the dark, and Joker is the one that is **humorous** and colorful. Pretty **ironic**, isn't it?

和小丑是有如「陰」和「陽」的完全相反。在大多數的故事中，英雄通常代表著「明亮」，而壞人代表「黑暗」。然而，在蝙蝠俠和小丑的情況下，則是相反的。蝙蝠俠是生活在黑暗中的那一個，而小丑則是代表幽默、豐富和多彩。頗諷刺，不是嗎？

卡漫精選字彙表

單字	詞性	中譯	單字	詞性	中譯
notable	*adj.*	顯著的	coma	*n.*	昏迷
unpleasant	*adj.*	使人不愉快的	brightness	*n.*	光明
venom	*n.*	毒液	humorous	*adj.*	幽默的
uncontrollable	*adj.*	無法管束的	ironic	*adj.*	具有諷刺意味的
paralysis	*n.*	癱瘓			

必考字彙大回顧

卡漫超給力字彙表

單字	中譯	詞性	反義字	反義字中譯
bleach	漂白	*v.*	darken	變暗
indication	指示	*n.*	misinformation	誤傳
comedian	諧星	*n.*		
robbery	搶劫	*n.*		
escape	逃脫	*v.*	capture	捕獲
disfigure	使……難看	*v.*	beautify	美化
terrorism	恐怖行動	*n.*		
extreme	極度的	*adj.*	insignificant	微不足道的
psychopath	精神病患者	*n.*		
penalty	懲罰	*n.*	award	獎賞
repeatedly	不停地	*adv.*	rarely	很少地
orderly	有條理的	*adj.*	disorderly	雜亂的
capable	有……能力的	*adj.*	clumsy	笨拙的
spectacle	公開	*n.*	hiding	藏匿
notable	顯著的	*adj.*	inconspicuous	不顯眼的
unpleasant	使人不愉快的	*adj.*	pleasant	愉快的
venom	毒液	*n.*	antidote	解藥
uncontrollable	無法管束的	*adj.*	manageable	可管理的
paralysis	癱瘓	*n.*		
coma	昏迷	*n.*	consciousness	有意識
brightness	光明	*n.*	darkness	黑暗

單字	中譯	詞性	反義字	反義字中譯
humorous	幽默的	*adj.*	**boring**	無聊的
ironic	具有諷刺意味的	*adj.*	**sincere**	真誠的

01 劃時代的傳奇

02 不朽的英雄神話

03 無堅不摧背後的英雄血淚

04 永存於人們心中的英雄霸主

MP3 19

The Birth of a Love Story and Wonder Woman
一個愛情故事和神力女超人的誕生

Once upon a time, there was a **native** to Paradise Island called the Amazon that was set in the middle of a vast ocean. On the island, there was a warrior princess known as Princess Diana of Themyscira. She was formed from clay by the Queen of the Amazons, and given life and power by four of the Greek and Roman gods.

Therefore, she is well-known as being as "Beautiful as Aphrodite, **wise** as Athena, **swifter** than Hermes, stronger than Hercules." She has strength that is comparable to Superman, and she is able to heal faster than normal human beings. She also is well-trained as a **masterful** athlete, **strategist**, and fighter.

從前，在廣闊的海洋中，有一個原始的天堂島稱為亞馬遜。在島上，有被譽為Themyscira的戴安娜戰士公主。她是由亞馬遜女王由捏陶而成型，由希臘和羅馬的四位神賦予了生命和力量。

因此，她因「美麗如阿芙羅黛緹，智慧如雅典娜，比愛馬仕快，比大力神強」而著名。她的實力是堪比超人，而她的自癒力也比一般人快。她還被訓練有素，成為一個出色的運動員，戰略家和鬥士。

A plane crash led to a **forbidden** relationship between Diana and Captain Steve Trevor. **Nursing** an **unconscious** man fostered the love. Diana didn't care and insisted to have a competition, a competition that will **determine** who is the strongest woman. Without a surprise, Diana won the competition and **convinced** her mother to return Steve Trevor back home. she was wearing the special dress made by her mother, and it was the Wonder Woman costume. The identity of Wonder Woman was born.

飛機失事使黛安娜和機長史蒂夫・特雷弗發展了禁忌關係。照料昏迷不醒的男人助長了愛情。戴安娜也沒在意，堅持參加比賽，一個決定誰是最強女人的比賽。毫無意外，戴安娜贏得了比賽，並說服她的母親，讓她帶史蒂夫・特雷弗回家。她穿著由她的母親所做的特別服裝，這是神力女超人的服裝。神力女超人的身份就此誕生。

01 劃時代的傳奇

02 不朽的英雄神話

03 無堅不摧背後的英雄血淚

04 永存於人們心中的英雄霸主

卡漫精選字彙表

單字	詞性	中譯	單字	詞性	中譯
native	adj.	天生的	nurse	v.	看護，護理
wise	adj.	有智慧的	forbidden	adj.	被禁止的
swift	adj.	快速的	competition	n.	競爭
masterful	adj.	威嚴的	determine	v.	決定
strategist	n.	戰略家	convince	v.	說服
unconscious	adj.	失去知覺的			

The Signature Weapons
標誌性的武器

Wonder Woman has a couple of signature weapons. The Lasso of Truth **compels** all human beings who come into contact with it to tell the truth.

神力女超人有幾個標誌性的武器。真理的套索，可以迫使接觸到它的人說出一切真相。

A pair of **indestructible** bracelets can block and **absorb** the impact of incoming attacks and eventually **deflect** automatic weapon fire.

一對堅不可摧的手鐲，可以阻擋和吸收攻擊進來的影響，並最終轉移力量成為自動武器。

She also has a magical sword that is sharp enough to cut the **electrons** off an **atom**.

她也有一把神奇且銳利的劍，使她可以削斷電子的原子。

The tiara allows her to **telepathically** contact people, and it can also be used as a throwing weapon.

后冠使她與人心靈感應，也可以作為投擲武器。

She travels with her invisible and silent plane which is also controlled by her amazing tiara.

她的旅行，也是由她驚人的后冠控制她的無形且無聲的飛機。

卡漫精選字彙表

單字	詞性	中譯	單字	詞性	中譯
compel	v.	強迫	electron	n.	電子
indestructible	adj.	不滅的	atom	n.	原子
absorb	v.	吸收	telepathically	adv.	心靈感應地
deflect	v.	轉向			

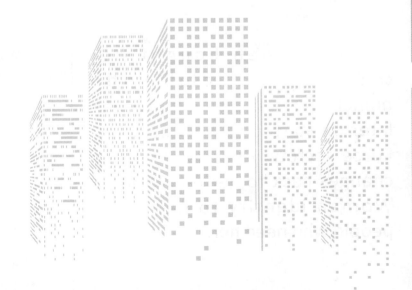

MP3 21

The Secret Identity – Diana Prince
秘密身份 － 黛安娜‧普林斯

To blend into the human world, Diana needed a new and **valid identity.**

She found this nurse that looked **identical** with her who wanted to leave for South America but didn't have enough money.

Diana then bought her **credentials** and started to live in the human world as Diana Prince. She later on started to work as an Air Force secretary but secretly, she changes back to her real Wonder Woman identity to help save people who need her.

為了融入人類的世界，戴安娜需要一個新的和有效的身份。

她發現了一個護士，看起來跟她很像。並想要離開去南美，但沒有足夠的錢。

戴安娜買了她的身份，並開始以黛安娜‧普林斯的身分生活在人類世界。後來她開始作為空軍的秘書，但暗地裡，她又變回她的真實神力女超人身份，以幫助拯救需要她的人。

People mostly describe Wonder Woman as the Superhero with **compassion** who gives love without **discrimination**.

She helps anyone in need and never accepts any reward. She is the **headstrong**, loving, and impregnable female role model.

人們大多是形容神奇女超人是有同情心的超人，給愛無歧視。

她幫助有需要的人，從不接受任何報酬。她是任性，有愛心和堅不可摧的女性榜樣。

卡漫精選字彙表

單字	中譯	詞性	單字	中譯	詞性
identical	*adj.*	相同的	discrimination	*n.*	歧視
credential	*n.*	憑據	headstrong	*adj.*	固執的
compassion	*n.*	同情憐憫			

必考字彙大回顧

卡漫超給力字彙表

單字	中譯	詞性	反義字	反義字中譯
native	天生的	*adj.*	auxiliary	輔助的
wise	有智慧的	*adj.*	foolish	傻的
swift	快速的	*adj.*	slow	慢速的
masterful	威嚴的	*adj.*	inferior	地位低下的
strategist	戰略家	*n.*		
unconscious	失去知覺的	*adj.*	awake	醒的
nurse	看護，護理	*v.*	ignore	忽視
forbidden	被禁止的	*adj.*	approved	批准了的
competition	競爭	*n.*	agreement	協議
determine	決定	*v.*	disprove	駁斥
convince	說服	*v.*	discourage	不鼓勵
compel	強迫	*v.*	dissuade	勸阻
indestructible	不滅的	*adj.*	breakable	易碎的
absorb	吸收	*v.*	exclude	排除
deflect	轉向	*v.*	straighten	弄直
electron	電子	*n.*		
atom	原子	*n.*		
telepathically	心靈感應地	*adv.*		
identical	相同的	*adj.*	distinct	不同
credential	憑據	*n.*		
compassion	同情憐憫	*n.*	animosity	敵意

單字	中譯	詞性	反義字	反義字中譯
discrimination	歧視	*n.*	**equity**	公平
headstrong	固執的	*adj.*	**tolerant**	寬容

01 劃時代的傳奇

02 不朽的英雄神話

03 無堅不摧背後的英雄血淚

04 永存於人們心中的英雄霸主

The Inner Voice Tells
內心的聲音說出

Instead of saying Cheetah is an enemy of Wonder Woman, it is more **suitable** to say that Cheetah is an identity that fights against Wonder Woman. It is because there is more than ONE Cheetah. There are actually FOUR of them including a male cheetah.

與其說豹女是一位神力女超人的敵人，也許更貼切地說，豹女是形容對戰神力女超人的一種身份。這是因為不只有一位豹女。事實上，他們有四人，包括一名男性的獵豹。

The first Cheetah was Priscilla Rich. She was a rich girl born with not only **aristocratic upbringing** but also a split of personality. She used to be the center of attention, but she was once being **eclipsed** by Diana Prince at a **charity** event.

第一位豹女是普席拉·瑞奇。她是個擁有貴族教養的富家女，但也有人格分裂。她曾經是人們關注的焦點，但她曾一度被神力女超人在一個慈善活動中搶走風采而黯然失色。

Priscilla tried to kill Diana at the

普席拉試圖在活

event, but she failed. There was then this inner voice telling her that the real her is the Cheetah, the **treacherous** and **relentless** Cheetah!

Priscilla battled with Wonder Woman several times, but never got a chance to kill her. Priscilla decided to retire to her North Shore Maryland mansion. She then passed away.

動中殺死戴安娜，但她失敗了。有個內心的聲音告訴她，真正的她是個豹女，奸詐，兇狠的豹女！

普席拉與神力女超人交手了幾次，但從來沒有殺死她的機會。普席拉決定在她北岸馬里蘭的豪宅退休。爾後，她離開了人世。

卡漫精選字彙表

單字	詞性	中譯	單字	詞性	中譯
suitable	*adj.*	適合的	charity	*n.*	慈善事業
aristocratic	*adj.*	貴族的	treacherous	*adj.*	背叛的
upbringing	*v.*	教育培養	relentless	*adj.*	無情的
eclipse	*n.*	蝕			

01 劃時代的傳奇

02 不朽的英雄神話

03 無堅不摧背後的英雄血淚

04 永存於人們心中的英雄霸主

MP3 23

Brain Washed Cheetah
被洗腦的豹女

The second Cheetah is a **precious** girl, Deborah, who decides to become an **ecology activist**. The head of the Villain's, Kobra captured her, **tortured** her, and brainwashed her to become his servant as a Cheetah. She even had several conflicts with Wonder Woman.

Only the 3rd and 4th Cheetah, Barbara Minerva and Sebastian Ballesteros have superpower. Dr. Barbara Minerva is an ambitious, selfish and **neurotic archaeologist** in England. During a visit to Africa, she searched out for **immortality**. Her powers were **conferred** to her by **ingesting** a combination of human blood and the berries or leaves of Urtzkartaga. Though, she

第二個豹女是個美麗的女子狄波拉，決定想當個生態學家。反派的眼鏡蛇龍頭捕獲她、折磨她、將她洗腦成他的奴隸。她甚至還與神力女超人有過一些衝突。

只有第三位和第四位豹女，獵豹，芭芭拉·密涅瓦和塞巴斯·巴列斯特羅斯有超能力。芭芭拉·密涅瓦博士是英國一位雄心勃勃但自私與神經質的考古學家。到非洲訪問期間，她搜索出丹藥。她的能力是來自注入人體血液

forgot one important requirement – being a virgin. Since Minerva was not, her **transformations** were part **curse** and part blessing. She experiences severe pain and physical **disability** in her human form and blood-thirsty **euphoria**, while in her cat form.

及Urtzkartaga的漿果或樹葉的組合。雖然，她忘了一件重要的要求 - 身為處女。由於密涅瓦不是處女，她的轉型成為部分詛咒及部分祝福，因為她在人形時經歷劇烈的疼痛和身體殘疾，而在她成為貓型時她則有著嗜血的快感。

卡漫精選字彙表

單字	詞性	中譯	單字	詞性	中譯
precious	adj.	可愛的	immortality	n.	不朽
ecology	n.	生態學	confer	v.	授與
activist	n.	行動主義者	ingest	v.	接納
torture	n.	拷打	transformation	n.	轉變
servant	n.	傭人	curse	v.	詛咒
conflict	n.	矛盾	disability	n.	無能
neurotic	adj.	神經質的	euphoria	n.	心情愉快
archaeologist	n.	考古學家			

01 劃時代的傳奇

02 不朽的英雄神話

03 無堅不摧背後的英雄血淚

04 永存於人們心中的英雄霸主

MP3 24

The One and Only
獨一無二

Even so, Barbara still wants to collect the Lasso of Truth. She tried all different kinds of ways to get the lasso without success.

即使如此，芭芭拉還是想要收集真理的套索。她嘗試了所有不同類型的方式來獲得套索，但沒有成功。

At their last battle, Diana's friend, Julia Kapatelis shot the Cheetah.

在他們的最後一戰中，戴安娜的朋友，朱莉婭·卡帕得利斯射殺了豹女。

The one and only male Cheetah, Sebastian Ballesteros was an Argentine businessman. He was also the lover of the Amazon's enemy, Circe.

唯一的一位男獵豹，塞巴斯·巴列斯特羅斯是位阿根廷商人。他也是亞馬遜的敵人，瑟茜的情人。

He convinced the plant god Urtzhartaga to convert him into the **supernatural** male Cheetah in order

他說服植物之神Urtzhartaga將他變成超自然的男性獵

to battle against Circe's enemy, Wonder Woman.

Because of his transformation, Barbara lost her Cheetah power. Barbara was furious. She **ultimately** killed Sebastian in his human form and regained her Cheetah form.

豹，以對抗瑟茜的敵人，神力女超人。

由於他的改造，芭芭拉失去了豹女的力量。芭芭拉大怒。她最終殺死了塞巴斯的人形，並恢復了豹女的形態。

卡漫精選字彙表

單字	詞性	中譯	單字	詞性	中譯
supernatural	*adj.*	神奇的	ultimately	*adv.*	最終

01 劃時代的傳奇

02 不朽的英雄神話

03 無堅不摧背後的英雄血淚

04 永存於人們心中的英雄霸主

必考字彙大回顧

卡漫超給力字彙表

單字	中譯	詞性	反義字	反義字中譯
suitable	適合的	*adj.*	inappropriate	不當的
aristocratic	貴族的	*adj.*	lower-class	低下階級
upbringing	教育培養	*v.*		
eclipse	蝕	*n.*	brighten	變亮
charity	慈善事業	*n.*		
treacherous	背叛的	*adj.*	loyal	忠誠的
relentless	無情的	*adj.*	compassionate	富於同情心的
precious	可愛的	*adj.*	disfavored	不受歡迎的
ecology	生態學	*n.*		
activist	行動主義者	*n.*	conservative	保守的
torture	拷打	*n.*	aid	援助
servant	傭人	*n.*	employer	雇主
conflict	矛盾	*n.*	consent	同意
neurotic	神經質的	*adj.*	rational	合理的
archaeologist	考古學家	*n.*		
immortality	不朽	*n.*	unimportance	不重要
confer	授與	*v.*	withhold	扣壓
ingest	接納	*v.*		
transformation	轉變	*n.*	stagnation	停滯
curse	詛咒	*v.*	blessing	祝福
disability	無能	*n.*	ability	能力
euphoria	心情愉快	*n.*	depression	消沉

單字	中譯	詞性	反義字	反義字中譯
supernatural	神奇的	*adj.*	usual	一般的
ultimately	最終	*adv.*	initially	原來

01 劃時代的傳奇

02 不朽的英雄神話

03 無堅不摧背後的英雄血淚

04 永存於人們心中的英雄霸主

MP3 25

 ### *Not The Stereotypical Superhero*
並非刻板印象的超級英雄

Different from most Superheroes, Baymax neither owns a killing outfit nor an incredible body nor an **unbeatable** power. He is a 75 inch high, 37 inch wide, **stout** and **squishy** white **vinyl** robot with extremely long arms. He is also the most **devoted**, **huggable**, **naive**, caring, selfless, **hospitable** and lovable robot anyone would ever see. He should match up to the described external image.

Baymax originally was only a **hydro-powered** robot programmed to be a personal health assistant. He was created by Tadashi Hamada

與大多數超級英雄不同，杯麵並不擁有一個超殺的裝備，一個令人難以置信的身體，也不具有無與倫比的力量。他是一個75英寸高，36英寸寬，一個具有極長的手臂，胖胖軟呼呼的白色塑料機器人。他也是所有人所見過最忠實，令人喜愛、天真、有愛心、無私、好客及可愛的機器人，他應該就符合所描述的外在形象。

杯麵原本只是一個被設計為水利驅動的個人健康助理機器人。他被Tadashi

as a healthcare providing robot nurse for the citizens of San Fransokyo. Tadashi himself was a brilliant scientist who wanted to create "something" to help improve **healthcare** around the world and for the **betterment** of humanity.

Baymax was given a special chip with Tadashi's **inscriptions**. No wonder he is as loveable and caring as Tadashi.

Hamada所創作出來，為San Fransokyo的公民提供醫療保健的機器人護士。Tadashi本人是一位出色的科學家，他想要發明可以幫助改善世界，並為人類改善醫療服務的「東西」。

杯麵被賦予擁有Tadashi銘刻的專用芯片，難怪杯麵竟然因此與Tadashi一樣的討人喜歡和貼心。

01 劃時代的傳奇

02 不朽的英雄神話

03 無堅不摧背後的英雄血淚

04 永存於人們心中的英雄霸主

卡漫精選字彙表

單字	詞性	中譯	單字	詞性	中譯
stereotype	*n.*	刻板	naïve	*adj.*	天真的
unbeatable	*adj.*	無敵的	hospitable	*adj.*	周到的
stout	*adj.*	矮胖的	hydro-powered	*adj.*	水力發電的
squishy	*adj.*	軟的	healthcare	*n.*	醫療保健
vinyl	*n.*	乙烯基	betterment	*n.*	改進
devoted	*adj.*	專心致志的	inscription	*n.*	刻文
huggable	*adj.*	令人喜愛的			

MP3 26

A Robot with Emotion and Personality
富有感情及人格的機器人

Even though Baymax is a calm robot, he needs time to think even under dangerous situations. Baymax often gets **distracted** by his **surroundings** owing to his **curiosity.**

It was not until he met Hiro that Baymax slowly begins to change and starts to have his own emotions and personality. Baymax used to treat Hiro as his patient, but little by little, Baymax started to feel a true emotional connection with Hiro.

When Hiro finds out his brother's death was not caused by an accident but was a murder by

杯麵是一個冷靜的機器人。即使在危險的情況下，他一樣需要時間去思考。也由於他的好奇心，杯麵常常會被他周圍的事務影響而分心。

杯麵在遇見了Hiro後開始慢慢的改變，並開始有了自己的情緒和個性。杯麵原本將Hiro當作自己的病人在對待，而一點一點的，杯麵開始對Hiro有了真正的情感聯繫。

當Hiro發現了他哥哥的死不是意外，而是被妖怪所害的一

Yokai, he gives Baymax an **upgrade** which includes a rocket fist. The super strength enables him to fight against rocket **thrusters** and allows him to fly.

Then, Hiro orders Baymax to murder Yokai. Baymax realizes that killing Yokai would not help Hiro, so he refuses to do so. He also **vows** to never harm a human being.

宗謀殺案,他讓杯麵升級,包括火箭拳頭、讓他可以飛對抗火箭推進器。

之後,Hiro下令杯麵去謀殺妖怪。杯麵意識到,殺害妖怪並不會幫助Hiro,因此他拒絕這樣做。他還發誓不會傷害人類。

卡漫精選字彙表

單字	詞性	中譯	單字	詞性	中譯
distract	*v.*	使分心	upgrade	*v.*	提升
surrounding	*v.*	周圍事物	vow	*v.*	發誓
curious	*adj.*	好奇的			

MP3 26 ▶

The Heartbreaking Sacrifice
令人心碎的犧牲

From the programming of Baymax, he will do anything to keep his **creator** away from any possible danger.

從杯麵的程式設定，他會想盡一切辦法讓他的創造者遠離任何可能的危險情況。

Thus, during a rescue trip, Baymax realizes that to **blast** Hiro to safety, sacrificing himself is the only way.

因此，救援之旅期間，杯麵意識到要將Hiro推向安全，犧牲自己是唯一的辦法。

Baymax calmly explains the situation to Hiro and **assures** that he will always be with him.

杯麵冷靜地說明了情況並要Hiro放心，他會一直陪在他身邊。

In tears, Hiro **deactivates** Baymax. Baymax **ignites** his rocket fist and sends Hiro back to safety while he is left **stranded** in the

Hiro以淚洗面的停用杯麵。杯麵點燃了他的火箭拳頭，送Hiro回到安全的地

sucking portal which eventually explodes.

Many people might not consider Baymax a superhero, but with his generous heart and fearless state of mind, I think he deserves the name of Superhero.

方，而他則無依無靠的留在了吸力門後，最終爆炸。

很多人可能不認為杯麵可以作為一個超級英雄。但他寬厚的心和無畏的智力，我覺得他應該得到超級英雄的名號。

卡漫精選字彙表

單字	詞性	中譯	單字	詞性	中譯
sacrifice	v.	犧牲	deactivate	v.	撤銷
creator	n.	創造者	ignite	v.	點燃
blast	n.	疾風	strand	v.	搓
assure	v.	擔保			

卡漫超給力字彙表

單字	中譯	詞性	反義字	反義字中譯
stereotype	刻板	*n.*	differentiate	區分
unbeatable	無敵的	*adj.*	vulnerable	弱勢的
stout	矮胖的	*adj.*	slender	苗條的
squishy	軟的	*adj.*	firm	硬的
vinyl	乙烯基	*n.*		
charming	迷人的	*adj.*	unattractive	沒有吸引力的
devoted	專心致志的	*adj.*	apathetic	麻木不仁的
huggable	令人喜愛的	*adj.*		
naïve	天真的	*adj.*	suspicious	可疑的
hospitable	周到的	*adj.*	incompatible	不相容的
hydro-powered	水力發電的	*adj.*		
healthcare	醫療保健	*n.*		
betterment	改進	*n.*	deterioration	惡化
inscription	刻文	*n.*		
distract	使分心	*v.*	clarify	澄清
surrounding	周圍事物	*v.*		
curious	好奇的	*adj.*	unconcerned	漠不關心的
upgrade	提升	*v.*	demote	降級
vow	發誓	*v.*		
sacrifice	犧牲	*v.*		
creator	創造者	*n.*		

單字	中譯	詞性	反義字	反義字中譯
blast	疾風	*n.*		
assure	擔保	*v.*	**veto**	否決
deactivate	撤銷	*v.*	**activate**	啟用
ignite	點燃	*v.*	**extinguish**	撲滅
strand	搓	*v.*		

01
劃時代的傳奇

02
不朽的英雄神話

03
無堅不摧背後的英雄血淚

04
永存於人們心中的英雄霸主

part 2

不朽的英雄神話

學習進度表

Unit 10 Yokai 妖怪
☐ 10-1 成長背景
☐ 10-2 微型機器人
☐ 10-3 邪惡計畫被揭穿
☐ 必考字彙大回顧

Unit 11 Elektra 幻影殺手
☐ 11-1 成長背景
☐ 11-2 失去對法律的信心
☐ 11-3 救贖
☐ 必考字彙大回顧

Unit 12 Kirigi 鬼摔
☐ 12-1 成長背景
☐ 12-2 權力腐化心智
☐ 12-3 徹底摧毀
☐ 必考字彙大回顧

Unit 13 Superman 超人
☐ 13-1 成長背景
☐ 13-2 另一個身分
☐ 13-3 致命弱點
☐ 必考字彙大回顧

Unit 14 Lex Luthor
雷克斯・路瑟
☐ 14-1 成長背景
☐ 14-2 渴望關注

☐ 14-3 智力天才
☐ 必考字彙大回顧

Unit 15 Iron Man 鋼鐵人
☐ 15-1 成長背景
☐ 15-2 祕密身分
☐ 15-3 超凡的裝備
☐ 必考字彙大回顧

Unit 16 Mandarin 滿大人
☐ 16-1 成長背景
☐ 16-2 新的啟發
　　　 激起更大的野心
☐ 16-3 隱形傳輸技術
☐ 必考字彙大回顧

Unit 17 Aquaman 水行俠
☐ 17-1 成長背景
☐ 17-2 維持海洋和平
☐ 17-3 無休止的報復
☐ 必考字彙大回顧

Unit 18 Black Manta
黑色曼塔
☐ 18-1 成長背景
☐ 18-2 出售自己的靈魂
☐ 18-3 絕佳狀態
☐ 必考字彙大回顧

是否能晉升為超能字彙英雄？

★完成10小節 →「肉雞小英雄」

★完成27小節 →「小小英雄達人」

★完成36小節 →「傳奇英雄」

MP3 28

The Death Leads to The Revenge
死亡導致復仇

As the head professor at the **prestigious** San Fransokyo Institute of Technology, Professor Callaghan was known for his **contributions** to **robotics**. He was not only a world – **renowned** scientist, but also the creator of Callaghan's Laws of Robotics. Callaghan was a loving man who wanted to change the world for the better. Tadashi Hamada and many other brilliant students **admired** him and regarded him as their **mentor.**

Callaghan used to have a daughter, Abigail, who was the love of his life. Abigail also was a **passionate** scientist, just like her father. She was working for the Krei Tech industries, the world

在San Fransokyo學院擔任教授主任的卡拉漢教授在對機器人技術的貢獻上是眾所皆知的。他不僅是一個世界知名的科學家，也是機器人卡拉漢定律的創造者。卡拉漢是一個有愛心的人並想讓世界變得更美好。Tadashi Hamada等眾同學傾慕他，並視他為自己的導師。

卡拉漢曾經有過一個女兒阿比蓋爾。她是他生命中的最愛。阿比蓋爾也是一個充滿熱情的科學家，就像她的父親一

leading technology industry owned by Alistair Krei.

様。她在撥爾高新技術產業工作。這個世界領先的技術產業是由阿利斯泰爾‧撥爾擁有。

There was a time that the company was developing a **revolutionized** transportation through the use of **portals.** They call the project: Silent **Sparrow.** Abigail was part of the test run. The disappearance of Abigail crushed Callaghan. Callaghan eventually lost himself and **descended** into **villainous** madness. The identity of Yokai was born.

曾經有一段時間，該公司正在開發革命性通過使用「門戶」的運輸。他們稱該項目為：雀無聲。阿比蓋爾是測試運作的一部分。阿比蓋爾的消失使得卡拉漢心碎。卡拉漢最終失去了自己，陷入了罪惡的瘋狂。妖怪的身份從此誕生。

卡漫精選字彙表

單字	詞性	中譯	單字	詞性	中譯
prestigious	*adj.*	有名望的	passionate	*adj.*	熱情的
contribution	*n.*	貢獻	revolutionize	*v.*	徹底改革
robotic	*adj.*	機器人的	portal	*n.*	入口
renown	*n.*	名聲	sparrow	*n.*	麻雀
admire	*v.*	欽佩	descend	*v.*	下降
mentor	*n.*	良師	villainous	*adj.*	惡棍的

MP3 29

The Unlimited Robot
無極限的機器人

During the San Fransokyo Tech exhibition, Hiro presented his great invention, "the Microbots". Hiro's original **intention** of using the Microbots was to help improve society's **efficiency**. Callaghan was very impressed by it and stole the first **generation** sample. Callaghan used the Microbots to fake his death and then integrated the **transmitter** into a mask used for his Yokai identity.

He also started to mass-produce the Microbots in order to **recollect** the missing pieces of the Silent Sparrow portal. Deep down, he still believes that his daughter is alive, but just **trapped** in an

在San Fransokyo科技展覽中，Hiro提出了他的偉大發明「微型機器人」。Hiro的原意是利用微型機器人來幫助提高社會效率。卡拉漢留下了非常深刻的印象，並偷走了它的第一代樣本。卡拉漢使用微型機器人來偽造他的死亡，然後將發射器置入他妖怪身份的面具裡。

他也開始大量生產微型機器人，為的是找回「門戶」中所消失的零件。在他的內心深處，他仍然認為他的女兒還活著，

unknown place.

Another mission Yokai had was to destroy Krei Tech as his revenge. Through his mask, he could transform the Microbots into anything in any form as he **desires**. During battles, Yokai could transform the Microbots into a deadly force. Without the kabuki mask and the Microbots, Yokai was **technically** powerless.

只是被困在一個不知名的地方。

另一個妖怪的任務是要摧毀揆爾高科技以達成復仇。透過他的面具，他可以依照他的希望，將微型機器人改造成任何形式。在戰鬥時，妖怪可以將微型機器人轉變成致命的力量。如果沒有歌舞伎面具和微型機器人，妖怪在技術上是無能的。

卡漫精選字彙表

單字	詞性	中譯	單字	詞性	中譯
intention	n.	意圖	recollect	v.	回憶
efficiency	n.	效率	trap	v.	落入圈套
generation	n.	世代	desire	v.	渴望
transmitter	n.	發射機	technically	adv.	技術上

01 劃時代的傳奇

02 不朽的英雄神話

03 無堅不摧背後的英雄血淚

04 永存於人們心中的英雄霸主

MP3 30

 The Turning Point
轉折點

Fortunately, one Microbot kept by Hiro was **reactivated** by Yokai and was trying to **reunite** with its kind.

幸運的是，有一個Hiro所保存的微型機器人被妖怪重新激活，並試圖與同類團聚。

Hiro and Baymax followed the Microbot and found out about Yokai's Microbots mass production.

Hiro和杯麵尾隨微型機器人並發現了妖怪的微型機器人量產計畫。

Yokai was very upset when he found out that his evil plan was exposed, so he used the Microbots to attack them.

當妖怪發現他的邪惡計劃被揭穿時，他很不高興，所以他用了微型機器人攻擊他們。

Hiro and the Big Hero 6 tried to remove the mask to rob him of his control over the Microbots. The kabuki mask was eventually

Hiro和大英雄6試圖卸下妖怪的面具以搶奪微型機器人的控制權。歌舞伎面具

destroyed by Hiro and Baymax.

最終被Hiro和杯麵銷毀。

卡漫精選字彙表

單字	詞性	中譯	單字	詞性	中譯
reactivate	*v.*	使恢復活動	**reunite**	*v.*	使再結合

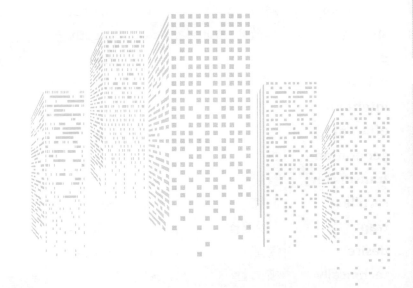

01 劃時代的傳奇

02 不朽的英雄神話

03 無堅不摧背後的英雄血淚

04 永存於人們心中的英雄霸主

必考字彙大回顧

卡漫超給力字彙表

單字	中譯	詞性	反義字	反義字中譯
prestigious	有名望的	*adj.*	insignificant	微不足道的
contribution	貢獻	*n.*		
robotic	機器人的	*adj.*	manual	手動的
renown	名聲	*n.*	obscurity	隱匿
admire	欽佩	*v.*	disrespect	不敬；無禮
mentor	良師	*n.*	student	學生
passionate	熱情的	*adj.*	dull	平淡的
revolutionize	徹底改革	*v.*	maintain	保持原狀
portal	入口	*n.*	exit	出口
sparrow	麻雀	*n.*		
disappear	消失	*v.*	appear	出現
slightly	輕微地	*adv.*	greatly	非常地
descend	下降	*v.*	rise	上升
villainous	惡棍的	*adj.*	respectable	可敬的
intention	意圖	*n.*		
efficiency	效率	*n.*		
generation	世代	*n.*		
transmitter	發射機	*n.*		
recollect	回憶	*v.*	forget	忘記
trap	落入圈套	*v.*	release	釋放
desire	渴望	*v.*	abhor	憎恨
technically	技術上	*adv.*		

單字	中譯	詞性	反義字	反義字中譯
reactivate	使恢復活動	*v.*	**deactivate**	關閉
reunite	使再結合	*v.*	**split**	分裂

Unit 11
Elektra 幻影殺手

11-1　成長背景

 MP3 31

The Tragic Childhood
悲劇的童年

The daughter of a Greek **ambassador**, Elektra Natchios was born on a Greek island near the Aegean Sea. Elektra's mother passed away right after Elektra was born. When she was nine years old, she was **assaulted** by kidnappers.

Luckily, she was rescued by her brother Orestez. She started to learn martial arts as an **adolescent**.

When she was 19, she traveled to the United States with her father and started studies in political science at Columbia University. During her school years, she met the love of her life, Matthew Murdock, who was blind but had superhuman sense.

希臘大使的女兒艾麗卡・納崔斯出生於靠近愛琴海的希臘島嶼。艾麗卡的母親在她出生後便去世了。在她九歲那年，她被綁架者毆打。

幸運的是，她被她的哥哥奧利特茲救出。她從青少年時期便開始學習武術。

在她19歲時，她與她的父親一同前往美國，並開始她在哥倫比亞大學的政治學研究。她在學校裡遇見了她這一生的摯愛，馬修・默多克。馬修是個盲人，但卻

擁有超能力。

A year later, Elektra and her father were held **hostage** by terrorists on campus. Matthew successfully saved Elektra, but her father was shot by the police by accident.

一年後，艾麗卡和她的父親在校園內被恐怖分子挾持。馬修成功地拯救了艾麗卡，但她的父親卻被警方意外地槍殺。

卡漫精選字彙表

單字	詞性	中譯	單字	詞性	中譯
ambassador	*n.*	大使	adolescent	*n.*	青少年
assault	*v.*	攻擊	hostage	*n.*	人質

MP3 32

Died in Lover's Arms
在愛人的懷裡死去

Elektra was crushed. She decided not to believe in the law, and she also left Matthew and the United States. Following a Sensei in Japan, she restarted her study in martial arts. She then joined a secret organization of martial artists which was led by Matthew's sensei, Stick. Her martial art skills improved **dramatically**, but due to the pain of losing her father, her soul is living in the darkness; thus, she was forced to leave the group.

She then started to follow the Hand who trained her as an assassin. She went back to New York City as a **bounty** hunter and assassin for many years. When she

　　艾麗卡心碎了。她決定不再相信法律，也離開了馬修和美國。她重新開始追隨一位日本老師，繼續她的武術學習。然後，她加入了由馬修的老師「施敵」所帶領的，武術家的秘密組織。她的門派技能顯著提高，但由於失去父親的痛苦，使她的靈魂活在黑暗中，因此，她被要求離開該團體。

　　爾後，她開始跟隨「魔掌派」。「魔掌派」將她訓練成一位刺客。她又再次回到紐約市，多年來成

found out that her old lover Matthew Murdock had become the Daredevil, even though he **vehemently opposed** her activities, she still cared deeply for him.

They eventually fought the Hand together, but Elektra's next boss, Wilson Fisk, ordered her to kill Matthew's best friend, Franklin Nelson. Elektra just couldn't do it. She was then killed by Bullseye. She died in her lover's arms.

為一位賞金獵人和刺客。當她發現她的舊情人馬修‧默多克已成為夜魔俠，儘管他強烈反對她的活動，她仍深深關心他。

他們最終一起打敗「魔掌派」，但艾麗卡的下一任老闆，威爾遜‧菲斯克，命令她殺死馬修最好的朋友，富蘭克林‧納爾遜。艾麗卡無論如何做不到這一點。她之後被「靶眼」殺害，在愛人的懷裡死去。

卡漫精選字彙表

單字	詞性	中譯	單字	詞性	中譯
ambassador	*n.*	大使	dramatically	*adv.*	戲劇性地
assault	*v.*	攻擊	bounty	*n.*	賞金
adolescent	*n.*	青少年	vehemently	*adv.*	激烈地
hostage	*n.*	人質	oppose	*v.*	反抗

Resurrection Gains Superpower
復活獲得超能力

Elektra was **resurrected** by a member of Stick's gang, but the order was given by the Hand. Thus, she again became the assassin.

She didn't **dare** to reveal herself to Matthew for years. As a ninja worrier, Elektra is familiar with **numerous** weapons such as the katana, ninja stars and throwing blades. But her trademark weapon are the twin sais.

After she was resurrected, she also gained a few superpowers. She started to be able to **manipulate** people's minds and made them see **illusions**. She also can control her own body functions, such as blood

艾麗卡被施敵的一位成員所復活，但卻是依循「魔掌派」的指使。於是，她又成為了刺客。

多年來，她不敢將她自己透露給馬修知道。作為一個忍者戰士，艾麗卡熟悉眾多武器，如武士刀、忍者星和投擲刀。但她的商標武器是她的兩隻三刃刀。

她復活後也獲得了一些超能力。她開始能夠操縱人們的思想，讓他們看到幻覺。她還可以控制自己的身體功能，如血

flow, heart rate. With the super powers she gained, she became even more battle **hardened**. Her **intense discipline** allows her to resist injury wounds.

So when she got a chance, she escaped from the Hand and allied with the S.H.I.E.L.D and the Avengers to fight crimes. Though, she still acts alone, and her ultimate goal is **REDEMPTION**.

液流動、心跳頻率等。隨著她獲得了超能力,她的戰鬥力變得更強。她強烈的自律讓她抵擋傷口的疼痛。

因此,當她有機會時,她從「魔掌派」中逃走,並與S.H.I.E.L.D和復仇者聯盟一起打擊犯罪。不過,她還是單獨行動,而她的最終目標是救贖。

卡漫精選字彙表

單字	詞性	中譯	單字	詞性	中譯
resurrect	*v.*	使復活	harden	*v.*	使變硬
dare	*aux,*	竟敢	intense	*adj.*	強烈的
numerous	*adj.*	許多的	discipline	*n.*	紀律
manipulate	*v.*	操縱	redemption	*n.*	贖回
illusion	*n.*	幻覺			

01 劃時代的傳奇

02 不朽的英雄神話

03 無堅不摧背後的英雄血淚

04 永存於人們心中的英雄霸主

必考字彙大回顧

卡漫超給力字彙表

單字	中譯	詞性	反義字	反義字中譯
ambassador	大使	*n.*		
assault	攻擊	*v.*	defend	保衛
adolescent	青少年	*n.*	adult	成人
hostage	人質	*n.*	captor	捕捉者
dramatically	戲劇性地	*adv.*	mildly	溫和地
bounty	賞金	*n.*	penalty	罰款
vehemently	激烈地	*adv.*	gently	平緩地
oppose	反抗	*v.*	accept	接受
resurrect	使復活	*v.*	destroy	破壞
dare	竟敢	*aux.*	abstain	避免
numerous	許多的	*adj.*	few	少數的
manipulate	操縱	*v.*	abandon	放棄
illusion	幻覺	*n.*	reality	現實
harden	使變硬	*v.*	soften	軟化
intense	強烈的	*adj.*	calm	冷靜的
discipline	紀律	*n.*	agitation	煽動
redemption	贖回	*n.*		

Unit 12
Kirigi 鬼摔

12-1　成長背景

MP3 34

The Best Warrior and Assassin with Mystery Background
最好的戰士與刺客的神秘背景

Possibly born in Japan, Kirigi's background is a **mystery**. Some people say that he is the son of the Hand's leader, Roshi, but it was never confirmed.

可能是出生在日本，鬼摔的背景一直是一個謎。有人說他是「魔掌派」領導者「羅西」的兒子，但從未被證實過。

He has been for years the best warrior and assassin. His **desperation** of becoming the leader of the criminal **association** makes him **pitiless** and cruel. He is willing to kill anyone who stands in his way.

他多年來一直是個最好的戰士和刺客。他成為犯罪團體首領的渴望使他無情與殘酷。他願意殺死擋住他去路的任何人。

Although Kirigi has normal **conscious** thoughts, he never speaks. Maybe that is why other ninjas are scared of him even more. Kirigi is also a ninja with super powers. His hands can be **consumed**

雖然鬼摔有正常意識及思想，他從來不說話。也許這就是為什麼其他的忍者們更懼怕他的原因。鬼摔也是有超能力的忍

with fire. He has the **resistance** to pain and injury, he has the power to lift at least 1,000 pounds, and he can also use **meditation** to recover from wounds. He is also a trained fighter who is able to fight with two katanas or even **unarmed**.

者。他的手可以起火，他有對痛和傷害的抵抗力，他擁有至少舉起1000磅的力量，他還可以使用冥想將他從創傷中恢復過來。他也是訓練有素的戰士，能夠利用兩個武士刀，甚至徒手與人戰鬥。

卡漫精選字彙表

單字	詞性	中譯	單字	詞性	中譯
mystery	*n.*	謎	consume	*v.*	花費
desperation	*n.*	絕望	resistance	*n.*	抵抗
association	*n.*	協會	meditation	*n.*	冥想
pitiless	*adj.*	無同情心的	unarmed	*adj.*	無武器的
conscious	*adj.*	神志清醒的			

The Deadly Order
致命的命令

When Roshi ordered Kirigi to kill Elektra, Roshi **assured** Kirigi that if he accomplishes the mission, he will become the leader of the Hand.

Kirigi was excited about the offer and set his mind to hunt Elektra down. Kirigi ordered a group of ninjas to **lure** Elektra and Daredevil to their secret hidden place. During the battle, Elektra **stabbed** Kirigi with her signature sias in the chest.

However, Kirigi is extremely powerful and was able to pull out the sias and continue the fight. Elektra again stabbed his chest with his sword. Kirigi was badly

當羅西下令鬼摔去殺害艾麗卡時，羅西承諾，如果鬼摔完成使命，他將成為「魔手派」的領袖。

鬼摔對這個提案感到亢奮，並誓言要抓到艾麗卡。鬼摔命令一組忍者去引誘艾麗卡與夜魔俠到他們祕密隱蔽的地方。在戰鬥時，艾麗卡用她的三刃刀刺傷了鬼摔的胸口。

然而由於鬼摔極為強大，他可以拔出三刃刀並繼續戰鬥。艾麗卡再次用鬼摔的劍刺進他的胸口。鬼

injured and ran off. Elektra thought she killed him.

摔因為重傷而逃跑，艾麗卡以為她殺了鬼摔。

卡漫精選字彙表

單字	詞性	中譯	單字	詞性	中譯
assure	*v.*	擔保	stab	*v.*	刺入
lure	*v.*	誘惑			

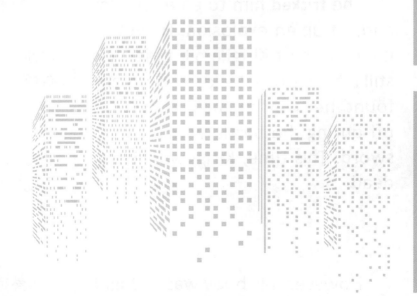

MP3 36

The Last Fight
最後一戰

However, Kirigi was able to find an **abandoned** church to meditate and heal his wounds. He once again tried to locate Elektra as soon as he was fully healed. Elektra was in shock when she found out Kirigi was still alive.

然而，鬼捽找到了一個廢棄的教堂，他利用默想醫治了他的傷口。當他完全癒合時，他再一次找到艾麗卡。當艾麗卡發現鬼捽還活著時，她被嚇壞了。

She **tricked** him to an empty lot and set up an explosion. However, it did not hurt Kirigi a bit. Kirigi was still after Elektra. Elektra eventually found her way to cut Kirigi's head off during the battle with his own sword. This time, Kirigi was finally dead.

艾麗卡騙鬼捽到一片空地，並企圖引爆他。但這一點都沒有傷害到鬼捽。鬼捽始終在追逐艾麗卡。艾麗卡最終找到了她的方式，在戰鬥中，用鬼捽自己的劍，砍下鬼捽的頭。這一次，鬼捽終於死了。

However, his body was brought

然而，他的遺體

back by the Hand and they successfully resurrected him. Kirigi was back to life! He then was sent to chase after Stick, Elektra, and the leader of the Chaste.

Kirigi found the Chaste's headquarters and tried to kill Stick, but he was tracked by several members of the Chaste and eventually killed by them. Kirigi's body was destroyed by the Stick this time so that he can no longer be brought back to life.

被運回「魔掌派」，他們成功地救活了他，讓鬼摔起死回生！他隨後被送去追逐施敵、艾麗卡和「貞潔」的領導者。

鬼摔找到了「貞潔」的總部，並試圖殺死施敵，但他被「貞潔」的幾名成員跟蹤，最終被他們殺害。鬼摔的屍體被施敵銷毀，並從此無法起死回生。

卡漫精選字彙表

單字	詞性	中譯	單字	詞性	中譯
abandon	*adj.*	被遺棄的	trick	*v.*	哄騙

01 劃時代的傳奇

02 不朽的英雄神話

03 無堅不摧背後的英雄血淚

04 永存於人們心中的英雄霸主

卡漫超給力字彙表

單字	中譯	詞性	反義字	反義字中譯
mystery	謎	*n.*	understanding	理解
desperation	絕望	*n.*	hopefulness	樂觀
association	協會	*n.*		
pitiless	無同情心的	*adj.*	merciful	仁慈的
conscious	神志清醒的	*adj.*	unconscious	無意識的
consume	花費	*v.*	accumulate	積累
resistance	抵抗	*n.*	surrender	投降
meditation	冥想	*n.*		
unarmed	無武器的	*adj.*	armed	武裝
assure	擔保	*v.*	deny	拒絕
lure	誘惑	*v.*	deter	阻止
stab	刺入	*v.*		
abandon	被遺棄的	*adj.*	keep	保持
trick	哄騙	*v.*	be honest	老實

MP3 37 ▶

The Last Survivor of Kypston
克利普頓星球的最後倖存者

"Faster than a speeding bullet. More powerful than a **locomotive**. Able to **leap** tall buildings in a single bound ... It's Superman!" This is the **formulistic** phrase when people describe Superman.

「比子彈更快，比火車更強大，能夠單一彈跳的躍上高層建築…他是超人！」這是當人們形容超人的制式化說法。

Born on the alien planet Krypton, Kal-El, A.K.A Superman, is the son of Jor-El and Lara. When his parents became aware of Krypton's **impending destruction**, Jor-El started to build a spacecraft that would carry Kal-El to Earth.

出生於克利普頓星球的凱·艾爾，又名超人，是喬·艾爾和拉拉的兒子。當他的父母知道克利普頓星球即將毀滅時，喬·艾爾開始建造一個可以將凱·艾爾帶到地球的太空船。

The spacecraft with Kal-El inside was **launched** right before Krypton exploded. His parents both died in the incident.

就在克利普頓星球爆炸前，載著凱·艾爾的太空船推進出發。他的父母均在事

件中死亡。

The spacecraft landed in country side of the United States. Jonathan and Martha Kent found the spacecraft and rescued Kal-El. They **adopted** the boy and renamed him Clark Kent.

太空船降落在美國的鄉村。喬納森和馬莎‧肯特發現了太空船並解救了凱‧艾爾。他們收養了這個男孩，並將他改名為克拉克‧肯特。

卡漫精選字彙表

單字	詞性	中譯	單字	詞性	中譯
locomotive	n.	火車頭	destruction	n.	毀滅
leap	v.	跳躍	launch	v.	發射
formulistic	adj.	公式化的	adopt	v.	領養
impending	adj.	逼近的			

MP3 38

The Unspeakable Super Powers
不可告人的超能力

During his growth, his adoptive parents discovered that Clark has superpowers. The Kent's taught Clark to **conceal** his origins and use the power **wisely** and responsibly. After Clark became a grown man, he created the **alter** ego of Superman with the red and blue costume with a letter "S" on his chest and a cape. As Clark Kent, he works for a newspaper, wears eyeglasses, loose clothing and suits and has a soft voice. As Clark Kent, he always avoids **violent confrontation**. Instead, he **slips** away and changes into Superman and then starts the rescue or the battle.

在他的成長過程中，他的養父母發現了克拉克的超能力。肯特夫婦教導克拉克要隱瞞他的出身，並明智且有責任地使用他的超能力。克拉克成年後，他創造了超人的服裝，利用紅色和藍色搭配裝束，並在他的胸前和披風上放了一個字母「S」。當是克拉克·肯特的身份時，他替報社工作，戴眼鏡，穿寬鬆的衣服和西裝，具有柔和的聲音。克拉克·肯特總是避免暴力對抗。相反的，當他溜走變成超人後，他則開始搶

Clark works for the Daily Planet and is **attracted** to his **colleague** Lois Lane. Ironically, Lois is attracted to Superman. There were times that Lois **suspected** Clark is Superman, but Superman never **admitted** the fact. As a hero from a planet that does not exist anymore and does not have any **survivors** besides him, Superman oftentimes feels lonely deep down.

救或戰鬥的行動。

克拉克在每日星球報工作，並被他的同事露伊絲‧蓮所吸引。諷刺的是，露伊絲喜歡的是超人。有幾次露伊絲懷疑克拉克就是超人，但超人卻從不承認這一件事。一個從已經不存在且沒有生還者的星球而來的英雄，超人內心常常感到孤單。

卡漫精選字彙表

單字	詞性	中譯	單字	詞性	中譯
conceal	v.	隱藏	attract	v.	吸引
wisely	adv.	聰明地	colleague	n.	同事
alter	v.	改變	suspect	v.	懷疑
violent	adj.	凶暴的	admit	v.	承認
confrontation	n.	對質	survivor	n.	生還者
slip	v.	滑動			

01 劃時代的傳奇

02 不朽的英雄神話

03 無堅不摧背後的英雄血淚

04 永存於人們心中的英雄霸主

MP3 39

The Power to Even Push Planets Around
甚至可以推行行星的超能力

Superman's signature powers include flight, super-strength, **invulnerability** to non-magical attacks, super speed, heat-**emitting**, super healing, super-intelligence and super-breath. He also has x-ray, heat-emitting, telescopic and microscopic vision. Actually, every superpower you can imagine, Superman has it.

He can even push planets around. He often time flies across the **solar system** to stop **meteors** from hitting the earth. He can also **withstand** nuclear blasts, fly into the sun, and survive in space without oxygen. Nothing can harm him, you might think. Actually, there is! Superman is the most

超人著名的能力包括飛行、超有力、對於非魔法的攻擊刀槍不入、超高速、可以發熱、超強的癒合、超級智能和超級氣流。他也有X光、發熱、伸縮和微觀的視野。其實，每一個你能想像的超能力，超人都有。

他甚至可以推行行星。他經常在整個太陽系飛行，以防流星隕石撞擊到地球。他也能承受核爆，飛入太陽，即使沒有氧氣也能在太空中生存。你可能會認為沒有什麼能傷害他。其

vulnerable to green Kryptonite radiation.

When Superman is exposed to to green Kryptonite radiation, his powers will be **nullified** and he will feel pain and **nausea**. It can eventually kill him. That might be his one and only weakness. With that being said, Superman is still considered the most powerful man on earth.

實有的！超人最容易受到綠色氪石輻射的傷害。

當超人暴露在綠色氪石輻射中時，他的能力將無用，他會感到疼痛和噁心，最終還會死掉。這也許是他唯一的弱點。即使是這樣，超人仍然被認為是地球上擁有最多超能力的人。

卡漫精選字彙表

單字	詞性	中譯	單字	詞性	中譯
invulnerability	*n.*	刀槍不入	withstand	*v.*	抵擋
emit	*v.*	發射	vulnerable	*adj.*	易受傷的
solar system	*n.*	太陽系	nullify	*v.*	使無效
meteor	*n.*	隕星	nausea	*n.*	噁心

01 劃時代的傳奇

02 不朽的英雄神話

03 無堅不摧背後的英雄血淚

04 永存於人們心中的英雄霸主

必考字彙大回顧

卡漫超給力字彙表

單字	中譯	詞性	反義字	反義字中譯
locomotive	火車頭	*n.*		
leap	跳躍	*v.*	drop	下降
formulistic	公式化的	*adj.*		
impending	逼近的	*adj.*	distant	遙遠的
destruction	毀滅	*n.*	construction	建造
launch	發射	*v.*	catch	抓住
adopt	領養	*v.*		
conceal	隱藏	*v.*	reveal	揭示
wisely	聰明地	*adv.*	foolishly	愚蠢的
alter	改變	*v.*	remain	保留
violent	凶暴的	*adj.*	gentle	溫和的
confrontation	對質	*n.*	consensus	共識
slip	滑動	*v.*		
attract	吸引	*v.*	disinterest	不關心
colleague	同事	*n.*		
suspect	懷疑	*v.*	trust	相信
admit	承認	*v.*	deny	拒絕
survivor	生還者	*n.*		
invulnerability	刀槍不入	*n.*	vulnerability	易受傷
emit	發射	*v.*	absorb	吸收
solar system	太陽系	*n.*		

單字	中譯	詞性	反義字	反義字中譯
meteor	隕星	*n.*		
withstand	抵擋	*v.*		
vulnerable	易受傷的	*adj.*	**invincible**	無敵的
nullify	使無效	*v.*	**validate**	使有效
nausea	噁心	*n.*		

Become the Best Scientist of the World
成為世界上最好的科學家

Lex Luthor is the son of Lionel and Letitia Luthor. He grew up in the **suburbs** of Smallville with his parents and sister, Lena. Despite the fact that he grew up on a farm, his **lifelong** ambition was to become the best scientist in the world.

The lab he used to own was a place where he could create many chemical solutions. However, during an experiment, he successfully created the **antidote** but accidentally knocked over a beaker and set the laboratory **ablaze**. Back then, his friend Superboy tried to use his super-breath to rescue him and save the lab.

雷克斯・路瑟是雷昂和利蒂希亞盧瑟的兒子。他與他的父母和姐姐莉娜在莫維爾鎮的郊區長大。儘管他在農場長大，他畢生的抱負是成為世界上最好的科學家。

盧瑟曾經有一個實驗室，當他還是小孩時，他就在那裡創造了許多化學解決方案。然而，在實驗中，他成功創建解藥，卻不小心打翻了一個燒杯，導致實驗室起火。當時，他的朋友超級小孩試圖用他的超級呼吸搶救他及實驗室。

However, Superboy mis-calculated. He successfully **extinguished** the fire, but accidentally destroyed Luthor's experiments and also his hair and left him completely **bald**. Luthor was furious. He **accused** Superboy of destroying his work on purpose because of **jealousy**. Since then, Luthor swore to **dominate** the earth and destroyed people with super powers.

然而，超級小孩錯估了情勢，他成功地撲滅了大火，但意外破壞了路瑟的實驗，也摧毀了他的頭髮，讓他成為完全的禿頭。路瑟大怒。他指責超級小孩因為嫉妒而目的性的摧毀他的作品。此後，路瑟發誓要主宰地球，摧毀擁有超能力的人。

卡漫精選字彙表

單字	詞性	中譯	單字	詞性	中譯
suburb	*n.*	近郊住宅區	bald	*adj.*	禿頭的
lifelong	*adj.*	終身的	accuse	*v.*	指控
antidote	*n.*	解藥	jealousy	*n.*	嫉妒
ablaze	*v.*	起火	dominate	*v.*	統治

01 劃時代的傳奇

02 不朽的英雄神話

03 無堅不摧背後的英雄血淚

04 永存於人們心中的英雄霸主

Shady Businessman, Successful Public Image
黑幕商人，成功的公眾形象

When he was 18, he met Clark Kent in Smallville and became friends with him. Years later, Luthor built his technology company, Lexcorp in Metropolis. Luthor was a **shady** businessman, but the business was very successful.

當他18歲時，他遇到超人克拉克・肯特，並與他交朋友。多年以後，路瑟建立了他的科技公司，雷克斯企業。路瑟是一個狡猾的商人，但生意非常成功。

He knows how to create public image and manipulate people's minds. He is well known for his **donations** to Metropolis over the years, funding **foundations** and charities. Luthor was considered the most powerful man in Metropolis. Luthor was even once **elected** president and found a position as part of the Justice League.

他知道如何建立公眾形象和操縱人心。他多年來捐贈給大都會的資助基金會和慈善機構的事是眾所周知的。路瑟被認為是大都會中最有權勢的人。路瑟甚至一度當選總統，並在正義聯盟裡有一席之地。

He was very happy and thought he had **achieved** his goal. But one day, he noticed that people started to put their focus in the sky. The attention he got from the public was all taken away by Superman. Superman also **accused** Luthor of his criminal behavior **publicly**. Luthor could not believe that this is the man that he became friends with years ago. He re-sets his goal to take down Superman and prove to the world that Luthor is the best.

他非常高興，以為他已經實現了他的目標。但是有一天，他發現人們開始把他們的焦點放在天空中。他從公眾那裡得到的關注都被超人帶走了。超人還公開指責路瑟的犯罪行為。路瑟簡直不敢相信這是幾年前成為他好朋友的人。他重新設定自己的目標要打倒超人並向世界證明了路瑟是最好的。

卡漫精選字彙表

單字	詞性	中譯	單字	詞性	中譯
shady	*adj.*	見不得人的	elect	*v.*	選舉
donation	*n.*	捐獻	achieve	*v.*	實現
foundation	*n.*	基金會	publicly	*adv.*	公然地

01 劃時代的傳奇

02 不朽的英雄神話

03 無堅不摧背後的英雄血淚

04 永存於人們心中的英雄霸主

MP3 42

 ## Represent the Opposite Humanity
反人類的代表

Different from Superman, Luthor is just a human, but an **intellectual** genius. He believes that with his intelligence, he is able to turn the world into a **Utopia**. Unfortunately, his **narcissistic** personality resulted in his lack of **empathy**. He is attributing all the mistakes to others, blaming Superman for always being the center of attention.

Luthor has been known to use weapons made of Kryptonite. He knows Kryptonite is the only thing that can hurt Superman. He also owns various battle suits which he created by himself. He wears his Warsuits **periodically** because they give him **enhanced** power and

　與超人不同，路瑟只是一個普通人，但卻是一個智力天才。他認為憑他的智慧，他能夠把世界變成一個烏托邦。不幸的是，他的自戀型人格導致他缺乏同情心。他將自己所犯的過錯推給別人，指責超人總是注目的焦點。

　路瑟使用氪石製成的武器已經是眾所皆知的了。他知道由氪石製成的武器是唯一可以傷害超人的武器。他還擁有自己所創作的各種戰鬥服。他週期性的穿著他的

advanced **weaponry** and other capabilities during battles.

Superman and Lex Luthor represent the two total opposites of humanity. Superman represents all the good and can achieve things that humanity could never **accomplish**, where Luthor represents the darkest side humanity can achieve.

「戰鬥服」，因為他們給他增強的力量，並備有先進的武器裝備和戰鬥中的其他功能。

超人和雷克斯·路瑟代表兩種完全相反的人性。超人代表所有的好，並且可以實現所有人類永遠無法完成的事情。反之，路瑟代表人性所能達到最黑暗的一面。

卡漫精選字彙表

單字	詞性	中譯	單字	詞性	中譯
intellectual	*adj.*	理智的	periodically	*adv.*	週期性地
utopia	*n.*	烏托邦	enhance	*v.*	提高
narcissistic	*adj.*	自戀的	weaponry	*n.*	武器
empathy	*n.*	同感	accomplish	*v.*	完成
existence	*n.*	存在			

必考字彙大回顧

卡漫超給力字彙表

單字	中譯	詞性	反義字	反義字中譯
suburb	近郊住宅區	n.	metropolis	都會
lifelong	終身的	adj.	temporary	臨時的
antidote	解藥	n.	poison	毒藥
ablaze	起火	v.	extinguish	撲滅
bald	禿頭的	adj.		
accuse	指控	v.	applaud	稱讚
jealousy	嫉妒	n.		
dominate	統治	v.	follow	跟隨
shady	見不得人的	adj.		
donation	捐獻	n.	hindrance	阻力
foundation	基金會	n.		
elect	選舉	v.		
achieve	實現	v.	fail	失敗
publicly	公然地	adv.	privately	私自的
intellectual	理智的	adj.	imbecile	傻子
utopia	烏托邦	n.		
narcissistic	自戀的	adj.	selfless	無私的
empathy	同感	n.	disdain	蔑視
existence	存在	n.	abstract	抽象
periodically	週期性地	adv.	irregularly	不規則
enhance	提高	v.	diminish	減少
weaponry	武器	n.		

單字	中譯	詞性	反義字	反義字中譯
accomplish	完成	*v.*	**begin**	開始

Two Master's Degrees at the Age of 15
15歲的雙碩士學位

The son of Howard and Maria Stark, Anthony Edward Stark was born on Long Island. Stark's father was a successful and wealthy **industrialist** and head of Stark Industries.

霍華德和瑪麗亞·史塔克的兒子，安東尼·愛德華·史塔克出生在長島。史塔克的父親是一個成功且富有的實業家和史塔克實業的老闆。

Stark himself was a genius who entered MIT at the age of 15 and received masters of electrical engineering and physics. Unfortunately, both of his parents were killed in a car accident. Since then, Anthony **inherited** his father's company.

史塔克是個天才，在15歲時進入麻省理工學院，並獲得電氣工程和物理學的碩士。不幸的是，他的父母在一場車禍中喪生。此後，安東尼繼承了父親的公司。

While Anthony was visiting Vietnam, he got injured by a **booby trap** and was captured by enemy

當安東尼訪問越南時，他因為詭雷而受傷，並被王秋所率

forces led by Wong-Chu. Wong-Chu **forced** Anthony to design and build weapons for him. Anthony refused.

He was badly injured. Luckily, he met a Nobel Prize-winning **physicist**, Ho Yinsen, in the prison.

領的敵軍所捕。王秋逼迫安東尼替他設計和建造武器。安東尼拒絕。

他受了重傷。幸運的是，他在監獄裡遇到了一位諾貝爾獎得主，物理學家何殷森。

卡漫精選字彙表

單字	詞性	中譯	單字	詞性	中譯
industrialist	*n.*	企業家	force	*v.*	強迫
inherit	*v.*	繼承	physicist	*n.*	物理學家
booty trap	*ph.*	圈套			

The Lifesaving Chestplate
救生裝甲

Yinsen made a **magnetic** chest plate to keep the **shrapnel** from reaching Anthony's heart in order to keep him alive. They also secretly built a suit of powered **armor** in order to **escape** from the prison. During the escape attempt, Yinsen sacrificed his life to save Anthony escape. After Anthony got home, he discovered that there is no way he could remove the shrapnel in his chest.

If he does, he will die. In order to live, he is forced to wear the armored chestplate **beneath** his clothes. The chestplate needs to be recharged every day. When Iron Man was discovered in public, Anthony told the public that Iron Man is just a robotic **personal**

　　殷森設計了一個具有磁性的裝甲，以防止砲彈碎片刺到安東尼的心臟。他們還偷偷內置動力裝甲，以利從監獄逃跑。在逃亡途中，殷森犧牲了自己的生命來拯救安東尼逃跑。安東尼回家後，他發現並沒有可以去除他的胸口砲彈碎片的方法。

　　如果他這樣做，他將會死亡。為了生活，他被迫在衣服裡穿著裝甲護胸。裝甲每天需要充電。當鋼鐵人在公共場所被發現時，安東尼告訴大家鋼鐵人只是一個機

bodyguard.

No one had any doubt about what Anthony had said because he **cultivates** a public image of being a rich playboy. Only a couple of people know his secret identity – his personal **chauffeur,** Harold "Happy" Hogan, and secretary Virginia "Pepper" Potts.

器人的貼身保鏢。

沒有人對安東尼有任何的質疑，因為他的公眾形象是一名富有的花花公子。只有幾個人知道他的秘密身份－他的私人司機哈羅德「快樂」霍根和秘書弗吉尼亞「辣椒」波茨。

卡漫精選字彙表

單字	詞性	中譯	單字	詞性	中譯
magnetic	*adj.*	磁性的	beneath	*prep.*	在……之下
shrapnel	*n.*	砲彈碎片	personal	*adj.*	個人的
armor	*n.*	盔甲	cultivate	*v.*	栽培
escape	*v.*	逃脫	chauffeur	*n.*	司機

MP3 45

Techno-Organic Virus Rewrites the Biology
生物有機病毒改寫生物特徵

Like Batman, he uses he personal fortune to fight against illegal activities, striving to be environmentally responsible. His heart condition was cured by an artificial heart transplant. Without any supehuman power, he simply relies on his designed weapons. The most standard one has been the repulsor rays, fired through the palms of his gauntlets. He also has the uni-beam projector in his chest, pulse blots, an **electromagnetic** pulse generator and a **defensive** energy shield. The bleeding edge armor is stored in Anthony's bones and can be assembled and controlled by his thoughts.

During a battle with the **extremis**-enhanced Mallen,

如同蝙蝠俠，他使用自己的財富來打擊犯罪活動，也努力對環境負責。人工心臟治癒了他的心臟問題。不具有任何超能力，他僅仰賴他所設計的武器。最制式的是衝擊光束，是透過手套的手掌上釋放。他也有在他的胸口設計單束光炮、電磁衝波發射器以及能量護盾。內層儲存裝甲被存在安東尼的骨骼中，可組裝並透過他的思想來控制。

在與絕境病毒強化後的敵手麥倫交戰

Anthony was badly injured. To survive, he injected his nervous system with modified techno-**organic** viruses which rewrote his biology. By doing so, he also gained an enhanced healing factor. He also is able to store some of the **components** of the armor-sheath in his body and can be recalled and **extruded** from his own skin.

後，安東尼受了重傷。為了生存，他在神經內注入改造過後的生化科技病毒，這改變了他的生物特徵。透過這樣做，他也得到了增強癒合的因子。他還能夠將部分裝甲的組件存儲在他的身體裡，並可以被調用，從他自己的皮膚中擠出。

01 劃時代的傳奇

02 不朽的英雄神話

03 無堅不摧背後的英雄血淚

04 永存於人們心中的英雄霸主

卡漫精選字彙表

單字	詞性	中譯	單字	詞性	中譯
loyalty	*n.*	忠心	durability	*n.*	耐久性
strive	*v.*	奮鬥	gauntlet	*n.*	交叉射擊
environmentally	*adv.*	有關環境方面	electromagnetic	*adj.*	電磁的
condition	*n.*	情況	defensive	*adj.*	防禦的
cure	*v.*	治癒	extremis	*n.*	緊要關頭
artificial	*adj.*	人工的	organic	*adj.*	有機的
transplant	*v.*	移植	component	*n.*	要素
allocation	*n.*	分配	extrude	*v.*	擠壓出

必考字彙大回顧

卡漫超給力字彙表

單字	中譯	詞性	反義字	反義字中譯
industrialist	企業家	*n.*		
inherit	繼承	*v.*	forfeit	喪失
booty trap	圈套	*ph.*		
force	強迫	*v.*	leave alone	不干涉
physicist	物理學家	*n.*		
magnetic	磁性的	*adj.*		
shrapnel	砲彈碎片	*n.*		
armor	盔甲	*n.*		
escape	逃脫	*v.*	capture	捕獲
beneath	在……之下	*prep.*	above	在……之上
personal	個人的	*adj.*	public	公共的
cultivate	栽培	*v.*	neglect	忽略
chauffeur	司機	*n.*		
loyalty	忠心	*n.*	disgrace	恥辱
strive	奮鬥	*v.*	dissuade	勸阻
environmentally	有關環境方面	*adv.*		
condition	情況	*n.*		
cure	治癒	*v.*	exacerbate	加劇
artificial	人工的	*adj.*	genuine	非偽造的
transplant	移植	*v.*		
allocation	分配	*n.*		

單字	中譯	詞性	反義字	反義字中譯
durability	耐久性	*n.*	**impermanency**	不持久的
gauntlet	交叉射擊	*n.*		
electromagnetic	電磁的	*adj.*		
defensive	防禦的	*adj.*	**offensive**	進攻的
extremis	緊要關頭	*n.*		
organic	有機的	*adj.*	**synthetic**	合成的
component	要素	*n.*		
extrude	擠壓出	*v.*	**pull**	拉

Mandarin 滿大人

16-1　成長背景

MP3 46

 Born Wealthy but Grew Up Penniless
出身豪門但長大後身無分文

Half Chinese and half English, Mandarin was born into a wealthy family in an **unnamed** village in mainland China before the **Communist** revolution.

一半是中國人，一半英國人，滿大人出生在一個共產革命前中國內的一個不知名村落的富裕家庭裡。

Even though Mandarin's father was considered one of the wealthiest people in China, he and his wife died soon after Mandarin was born.

儘管滿大人的父親被認為是最富有的中國人之一，他和他的妻子在滿大人出生後不久就去世了。

Mandarin was raised by his **radical** aunt who was **embittered** against the world.

滿大人是由他反世界的激進派阿姨所帶大。

She spent every bit of the family fortune training Mandarin in science and **combat**. Mandarin became the master of what he has

她花了家裡的每一分財產，在科學和格鬥上培訓滿大人。滿大人成為了這方面

learned, but was **penniless** and unable to pay his taxes. Therefore, Mandarin was **evicted** from his own house by the government.

的菁英，但卻身無分文，無力支付稅金。因此，滿大人被政府驅逐出自己的房子。

卡漫精選字彙表

單字	詞性	中譯	單字	詞性	中譯
unnamed	*adj.*	未命名的	combat	*n.*	格鬥
communist	*n.*	共產主義者	penniless	*adj.*	身無分文的
radical	*adj.*	根本的	evict	*v.*	逐出
embitter	*v.*	使難受			

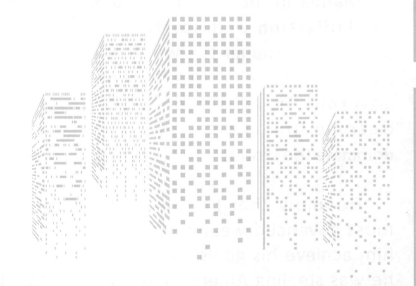

MP3 47

Start the Journey to Conquer the World
啟程征服世界

Having no place to go, Mandarin decided to explore the forbidden Valley of Spirits where no one has visited for centuries. He spent years there studying Makluan science and learning how to use the ten rings he found within the starship of Axonn-Karr.

Mandarin then returned back to **civilization** and started his journey to **conquer** the world. He swore he will crash the government, kill the ones who despise him, and eventually **dominate** the world.

He knew that he needs the most advanced weapons to help him achieve his goals. Therefore, he was stealing American **missiles**

無路可去,滿大人決定探索幾百年來從未有人走訪的禁谷。他花了幾年,學習麥卡倫科學,學習如何使用他在艾森卡爾的飛船內發現的十枚戒指。

滿大人爾後返回文明,開始了他的旅程,征服世界。他發誓他要擊潰政府,殺死每一個曾經看不起他的那些人,並最終統一天下。

他知道,他需要最先進的武器,以幫助他實現他的目標。因此,他偷了由安東

and spy planes built by Anthony Stark. Of course Anthony could not let Mandarin **ruin** his **reputation**. He never wants his developments to be used for no good. So he put on his Iron Man armor to **investigate** in China. Since then, Iron Man became Mandarin's number one enemy against his plans to take over the world.

尼・史塔克在美國製造的導彈和間諜飛機。當然，安東尼不能讓滿大人毀了他的名聲。他從來不希望自己的發明是用在無益的地方。於是，他利用他鋼鐵人的盔甲在中國進行調查。此後，鋼鐵人成了滿大人心中反對他接管世界計劃的頭號敵人。

卡漫精選字彙表

單字	詞性	中譯	單字	詞性	中譯
conquer	v.	征服	ruin	v.	毀滅
civilization	n.	文明	reputation	n.	名聲
dominate	v.	統治	investigate	v.	調查
missile	n.	飛彈			

01 劃時代的傳奇
02 不朽的英雄神話
03 無堅不摧背後的英雄血淚
04 永存於人們心中的英雄霸主

The Battles Between Iron Man and Mandarin
鋼鐵人和滿大人之間的鬥爭

Mandarin then used the **teleportation** technology from Makluan science to kidnap Swordsman to destroy the Avengers. However, he was **betrayed** by Swordsman. Mandarin then teleported Harold "Happy" Hogan to his castle in China. Harold was wearing the Iron Man armor at that time to protect Anthony's secret identity. Mandarin thought he had captured the real Iron Man. In rescuing Hogan, Iron Man **bested** for the first time! Iron Man then destroyed Mandarin's castle. Although, Mandarin escaped with his teleportation **machinery**, he then created a device that **broadcasts** "hate-rays" toward Earth.

滿大人利用馬卡倫科學的隱形傳輸技術，綁架了劍士，以摧毀復仇者聯盟。然而，他被劍士所出賣。滿大人爾後傳輸了哈羅德「快樂」霍根，並將他關在他中國的城堡中。哈羅德當時為了保護安東尼的秘密身份身穿著鋼鐵人的盔甲。滿大人以為他已經抓住了真正的鋼鐵人。在搶救霍根時，鋼鐵人第一次擊敗了滿大人！鋼鐵人之後毀了滿大人的城堡。雖然滿大人利用他的隱形傳輸逃脫了。之後，他創造了「仇恨射線」，並

將之射向地球。

There was a time that Mandarin shifted his attention to Hulk, hoping he could help him take over the world. He then **allied** with Sandman. Mandarin then attacked Iron Man by employing an **android** in the Hulk's likeness. Mandarin also set up a **makeshift** base of operations in order to discredit Stark **publicly**. Mandarin tried to find out if Iron Man is actually Stark while he was holding him in **custody** for the fourth time, but he still couldn't find out the truth. Mandarin then tried to kill Stark's girlfriend, Janice Cord.

曾經有段時間他將注意力轉向浩克，希望他能幫他接管世界。隨後，他與沙人結盟。之後滿大人再利用與浩克相似的機器人攻擊鋼鐵人。滿大人還設置了操作的臨時基地，以公開抹黑史塔克。滿大人試圖找出鋼鐵人，但其實就是史塔克。而他在第四次羈押他時還是沒能找出真相。然後滿大人試圖殺死史塔克的女友，珍妮絲·科德。

卡漫精選字彙表

單字	詞性	中譯	單字	詞性	中譯
confront	v.	面臨；遭遇	broadcast	v.	播送
captive	n.	俘虜	ally	v.	結盟
teleportation	n.	遠距離即時傳送	android	adj.	有人類特徵的
betray	v.	背叛	makeshift	n.	權宜之計
best	v.	勝過	publicly	adv.	公開地
machinery	n.	機械	custody	n.	監護

必考字彙大回顧

卡漫超給力字彙表

單字	中譯	詞性	反義字	反義字中譯
unnamed	未命名的	*adj.*	named	命名的
communist	共產主義者	*n.*	capitalist	資本家
radical	根本的	*adj.*	inessential	非必要性的
embitter	使難受	*v.*	calm	使冷靜
combat	格鬥	*n.*	surrender	投降
penniless	身無分文的	*adj.*	wealthy	富裕的
evict	逐出	*v.*	keep	保持
conquer	征服	*v.*	give in	讓步
civilization	文明	*n.*	barbarism	野蠻
dominate	統治	*v.*	obey	遵守
missile	飛彈	*n.*		
ruin	毀滅	*v.*	heal	癒合
reputation	名聲	*n.*		
investigate	調查	*v.*		
confront	面臨；遭遇	*v.*	dodge	躲閃
captive	俘虜	*n.*		
teleportation	遠距離即時傳送	*n.*		
betray	背叛	*v.*	loyal	忠誠
best	勝過	*v.*	lost	失去

單字	中譯	詞性	反義字	反義字中譯
machinery	機械	*n.*		
broadcast	播送	*v.*	**secret**	秘密
ally	結盟	*v.*	**enemy**	敵人
android	有人類特徵的	*adj.*		
makeshift	權宜之計	*n.*		
publicly	公開地	*adv.*	**privately**	私人的
custody	監護	*n.*		

01 劃時代的傳奇

02 不朽的英雄神話

03 無堅不摧背後的英雄血淚

04 永存於人們心中的英雄霸主

The Discovery of Atlantis
亞特蘭蒂斯的發現

Born by the ocean, Arthur Curry is the son of Tom Curry, a lighthouse keeper, and Atlanna. Atlanna passed away when Arthur was a baby.

His father, Tom, spent most of his time underwater as an undersea **explorer**.

He found an **ancient** city in the **depths** where no one had ever **penetrated**. He believed it was the lost kingdom of Atlantis. Tom then spent most of his time in one of the palaces.

In the palace, he found a lot of

出生於海邊，亞瑟‧柯瑞是看守燈塔者湯姆‧柯瑞和亞特蘭那的兒子。亞特蘭那去世時，亞瑟還是個嬰兒。

他的父親湯姆，花了他大部分時間在海底探險。

他發現了一個古老的城市，在沒有人滲透的深處。他認為，這是亞特蘭蒂斯的失落王國。湯姆當時花了他的大部分時間在其中一個宮殿之中。

在宮中，他發現

books and records which taught him ways to live under the ocean. Tom also trained Arthur ways to live and **thrive** under the water.

了大量的書籍和記錄，這些文獻教會他如何在海洋底下生活。湯姆也教育亞瑟在水底生活的方式，並在水中茁壯成長。

卡漫精選字彙表

單字	詞性	中譯	單字	詞性	中譯
explorer	*n.*	探險家	**penetrate**	*v.*	滲透
ancient	*adj.*	古代的	**thrive**	*v.*	繁榮
depth	*n.*	深度			

Born to Be Aquaman
天生的水行俠

He has the ability to live in the depths of the ocean, breathe underwater, remain **unaffected** by the **immense** pressure and the cold temperatures of the ocean. He can also swim at the speed of 3,000 meters per second and can swim up Niagara Falls. He even withstands gun fire, sees in darkness and can hear limited **sonar**.

Besides all that, Arthur's most **recognized** power is the **telepathic** ability to communicate with anything related to the ocean, whether it's **underneath** or upon the sea. He is also capable of gathering all sea related lives together as a whole. Arthur eventually decided to use his

他可以住在海洋深處,在水裡呼吸,並且不會受到巨大的壓力和海洋低溫的影響。他還可以以每秒3000米的速度游泳,並逆游尼亞加拉大瀑布。他也可以防彈,在黑暗中看到事物,並可以聽到有限的聲納。

除了這一切,亞瑟最被認可的能力是與跟海洋有關的任何東西溝通,無論是否是在海上或海中的任何東西做心靈的感應。他還能集合海中生物,作為一個整體。亞瑟最終決定用

power to help keep the oceans in peace. He started to name himself Aquaman.

Although he can remain underwater for **unlimited** time, Aquaman cannot remain on land for over one hour. Fortunately, when he met Batman, Batman invented a water suit for Aquaman so he is able to stay on land for an **indefinite** amount of time.

自己的力量來幫助維持海洋和平。他開始叫自己水行俠。

雖然他可以無時間限制的待在水中，但水行俠不能在陸地上待超過一小時。幸運的是，當他遇到蝙蝠俠時，蝙蝠俠發明了一套水裝，讓水行俠能夠時間不限地留在陸地上。

卡漫精選字彙表

單字	詞性	中譯	單字	詞性	中譯
unaffected	*v.*	未被影響的	telepathic	*adj.*	精神感應的
immense	*adj.*	巨大的	underneath	*prep.*	在⋯⋯下面
sonar	*n.*	聲納	unlimited	*adj.*	無限制的
recognize	*v.*	認出	indefinite	*adj.*	不確定的

Grudge and Jealousy Breed Murder
仇恨和嫉妒所引起的殺機

Aquaman battled with several sea-based **villains**, including Nazi U-boat commanders, modern-day pirates, and many **threats** to **aquatic** life. But his biggest enemies must be Black Manta and Orm Curry. Black Manta was ordered to collect the blood of Arthur Curry to prove that he was actually an Atlantean. He failed in the mission and later on his father was killed by Aquaman.

Black Manta held a grudge against Aquaman and started an endless revenge. On the other hand, Orm Curry who is Aquaman's half-brother grew up as the trouble maker and lived in the **shadow** of his brother. Since Tom Curry's

與水行俠交手的幾個海基惡棍，其中包括了納粹潛艇指揮官、現代海盜以及水生生物的許多威脅。但他最大的敵人必定是黑色曼塔和奧姆·柯瑞。黑色曼塔奉命收集亞瑟·柯瑞的血來證明他確實是亞特蘭蒂斯的一員。他的任務失敗，他的父親也被水行俠所殺害。

黑色曼塔痛恨水行俠，並開始了無休止的報復。另一方面，奧姆·柯瑞是水行俠同父異母的弟弟，一個成長在哥哥影子裡的麻煩製造

mother is an ordinary woman, he does not possess any superhuman strength.

者。因為湯姆‧柯瑞的母親是普通人類，他不具有任何超能力特質。

His jealousy toward Aquaman led him to become Aquaman's **nemesis**, Ocean Master.

他對水行俠的忌妒導致他成了水行俠的剋星，海洋大師。

卡漫精選字彙表

單字	詞性	中譯	單字	詞性	中譯
villain	*n.*	惡棍	shadow	*n.*	陰影
threat	*n.*	威脅	ordinary	*adj.*	平常的
aquatic	*adj.*	水棲的	nemesis	*n.*	復仇者

01 劃時代的傳奇

02 不朽的英雄神話

03 無堅不摧背後的英雄血淚

04 永存於人們心中的英雄霸主

必考字彙大回顧

卡漫超給力字彙表

單字	中譯	詞性	反義字	反義字中譯
explorer	探險家	*n.*		
ancient	古代的	*adj.*	modern	現代的
depth	深度	*n.*	height	高度
penetrate	滲透	*v.*		
thrive	繁榮	*v.*	laggard	落後的
unaffected	未被影響的	*v.*	affected	受影響的
immense	巨大的	*adj.*	tiny	微小的
sonar	聲納	*n.*		
recognize	認出	*v.*		
telepathic	精神感應的	*adj.*	physical	身體的
underneath	在……下面	*prep.*	above	在……以上
unlimited	無限制的	*adj.*	limited	有限的
indefinite	不確定的	*adj.*	definite	確定的
villain	惡棍	*n.*	hero	英雄
threat	威脅	*n.*		
aquatic	水棲的	*adj.*		
shadow	陰影	*n.*		
ordinary	平常的	*adj.*	abnormal	不正常的
nemesis	復仇者	*n.*		

MP3 52

Tragic Childhood Causes Deviant Behavior
悲劇的童年導致越軌行為

On an ordinary day, while a sea-loving boy in Baltimore was enjoying his day by the ocean, he was kidnapped by some guys. He was enslaved on a ship, feeling so hopeless until he saw Aquaman and his dolphin friends. The little boy sent many signals to Aquaman expecting his rescue, but his hope was shattered because Aquaman didn't see him. He started to hate the ocean and Aquaman, resolving to become the master of the sea. After he grew up, he became a **ruthless** treasure hunter and **mercenary**. He designed his own wetsuit with a bug-eyed helmet which can shoot **blasting** rays from its eyes. He also started to call himself Black Manta. During most of his time, he **scavenges** the

在巴爾的摩的一個平凡日子，一位熱愛海洋的小男孩正在海邊享受他的時光，他被幾個人綁架了。他在船上被迫做奴役的工作，感到希望渺茫，直到他看見水行俠和他的海豚朋友。小男孩傳遞許多訊號給水行俠，期待他的救援，但卻希望破滅，因為水行俠沒看見他。他開始討厭海洋和水行俠，下定決心要成為大海的主人。他長大後，成為了一個無情的尋寶獵人和傭兵。他設計了自己的潛水衣與有著如蟲眼讓他可以發射

explores depths of the ocean trying to find the long lost **relics** and powerful **mythical** items. One time, he was hired by Stephen Shin to collect a sample of Arthur Curry's blood. Black Manta initiated an attack while Arthur and his father were out at the sea. Although his father, Tom Curry, fought back, he **suffered** from a heart attack and **ultimately** died. Aquaman's revenge later on accidentally killed Black Manta's father, resulting in the circle of vengeance.

爆破射線的鋼盔。他也開始稱自己為黑色曼塔。在他的大部分時間裡，他在海洋裡拾荒，試圖尋找失蹤多年的文物和強大的神話寶物。有一次，他被史蒂芬・辛聘請收集亞瑟・柯瑞的血液樣本。黑色曼塔在亞瑟和他的父親出海時發起攻擊他們。雖然他的父親湯姆・柯瑞，展開反擊，但因心臟病發最終死亡。水行俠稍後復仇，在意外之下水行俠失手殺死了黑色曼塔的父親，復仇的輪迴從此開始。

01 劃時代的傳奇

02 不朽的英雄神話

03 無堅不摧背後的英雄血淚

04 永存於人們心中的英雄霸主

卡漫精選字彙表

單字	詞性	中譯	單字	詞性	中譯
deviant	*adj.*	越軌的	scavenge	*v.*	在…中搜尋
vengeance	*n.*	報仇	relic	*n.*	遺物
ruthless	*adj.*	無情的	mythical	*adj.*	神話的
mercenary	*adj.*	圖利的	suffer	*v.*	遭受
blasting	*n.*	爆炸	ultimate	*adj.*	最後的

Unit 18
Black Manta 黑色曼塔

18-2 出售自己的靈魂

 The Death of Aquababy
水寶寶的死

Manta first kidnapped Aquaman's wife, Mera, and their baby, Aquababy. He **defeated** Aquaman and turned him over to King Karshon. He then killed Aquababy in front of Aquaman.

曼塔首先綁架了水行俠的妻子梅拉，和他的寶貝，水寶寶。他擊敗了水行俠並且把他交給凱森國王。然後，他在水行俠面前殺死了水寶寶。

Aquaman was sad and angry. He hunted Manta down and nearly killed him. Instead, he decided to turn him over to the **authorities**. When Manta was released, he didn't regret anything he had done. Although, he gave up his thought on taking Aquaman down.

水行俠既難過又生氣。他捉到曼塔，且幾乎殺了他。然而，他決定把他交給當局。曼塔被釋放時，他對自己所做的事情並不後悔。雖然，他放棄了打敗水行俠的想法。

Instead, Manta agreed to sell his soul to Neron for power and

反之，曼塔同意將他靈魂出售給內隆

started to do drug **smuggling** and some shady works in Star City. Manda even approached Aquaman to work with him.

以得到能力，並開始做毒品走私，並在星城裡做一些見不得人的事。曼達甚至找上水行俠與他合作。

Of course Aquaman wouldn't agree. Black Manda then attacked Sub Diego and nearly killed Captain Marley. Aquaman set several **predatory** forms of sea-life on him to kill him. Black Manda used an electrical charge in his suit to **fend** off his attackers and somehow managed to survive.

當然了，水行俠不會同意。黑色曼塔隨後攻擊了狄亞哥，並險些殺死馬利隊長。水行俠爾後在海上設置了幾種形式，企圖殺了他。黑色曼達在他的衣服裡設計了電荷用來抵擋他的攻擊者，總算生存下來。

卡漫精選字彙表

單字	詞性	中譯	單字	詞性	中譯
defeat	*v.*	戰勝	predatory	*adj.*	掠奪成性的
authority	*n.*	權力	fend	*v.*	抵擋
smuggle	*v.*	走私			

01 劃時代的傳奇

02 不朽的英雄神話

03 無堅不摧背後的英雄血淚

04 永存於人們心中的英雄霸主

A Regular Human Being with Great Gadgets
擁有超級工具的普通人

Different from Aquaman, Black Manta was not born with powers or abilities. He was gifted with great leadership and was a skilled strategist. He is also a gifted **manipulator**. Though he trained himself to become expert in various things, such as diving, treasure hunting, assassinations and fighting, he forces himself to always maintain the best physical condition.

He is also a very good mechanical engineer. He designs a large **arsenal** of weapons, equipment and vehicles. And his greatest invention must be his diving suit which **enables** him to survive underwater regardless of the depths, the temperature, and

不同於水行俠，黑色曼塔不具有與生俱來的權力或能力。他擁有與生俱來的領導能力且是熟練的戰略家。他也是一個天才的操縱者。他訓練自己做各種事情，如潛水尋寶，當刺客和戰鬥。他還強迫自己始終保持最佳的身體狀態。

他也是一個很好的機械工程師。他設計了大型軍火庫武器、設備和車輛。而他最偉大的發明一定就是他的潛水服。這使他在水下無論多少深度、溫度和壓力都

pressure. It is also waterproof and bullet proof. The signature manta-shaped helmet with two large eyes allows him to have **scope** vision and powerful optic blasts that are capable of hurting others. The helmet also connects to an oxygen system which allows him to breathe underwater.

能生存。它防水也防彈。兩個大眼睛的蝠形頭盔讓他有大範圍的視線和足以傷害人的強大光束。頭盔還連接到一個氧氣系統，允許他在水下呼吸。

卡漫精選字彙表

單字	詞性	中譯	單字	詞性	中譯
manipulator	*n.*	操作者	enable	*v.*	使能夠
arsenal	*n.*	兵工廠	scope	*n.*	範圍

必考字彙大回顧

卡漫超給力字彙表

單字	中譯	詞性	反義字	反義字中譯
deviant	越軌的	*adj.*	standard	標準的
expect	預計……可能發生	*v.*	disregard	漠視
vengeance	報仇	*n.*	forgiveness	饒恕
ruthless	無情的	*adj.*	compassionate	富於同情心的
mercenary	圖利的	*adj.*	altruistic	利他的
blasting	爆炸	*n.*		
scavenge	在…中搜尋	*v.*		
relic	遺物	*n.*		
mythical	神話的	*adj.*	factual	事實的
suffer	遭受	*v.*	abstain	避免
ultimate	最後的	*adj.*	beginning	開始的
defeat	戰勝	*v.*	lose	戰敗
authority	權力	*n.*		
smuggle	走私	*v.*		
predatory	掠奪成性的	*adj.*		
fend	抵擋	*v.*	open	打開
manipulator	操作者	*n.*		
arsenal	兵工廠	*n.*		
enable	使能夠	*v.*	prevent	避免
scope	範圍	*n.*		

part3
無堅不摧背後的英雄血淚

學習進度表

Unit 19 Thor 雷神索爾
□ 19-1 成長背景
□ 19-2 忌妒心
□ 19-3 超凡的能力
□ 必考字彙大回顧

Unit 20 Loki 洛基
□ 20-1 成長背景
□ 20-2 摧毀雷神和掌控仙宮
□ 20-3 魔藥
□ 必考字彙大回顧

Unit 21 Green Lantern 綠光戰警
□ 21-1 成長背景
□ 21-2 受女人寵愛的男人
□ 21-3 重新點燃太陽
□ 必考字彙大回顧

Unit 22 Sinestro 賽尼斯托
□ 22-1 成長背景
□ 22-2 鐵腕統治
□ 22-3 黃色能源戒指
□ 必考字彙大回顧

Unit 23 The Thing 石頭人
□ 23-1 成長背景
□ 23-2 秘密飛行
□ 23-3 賦予的能力
□ 必考字彙大回顧

Unit 24 Dr. Doom 末日博士
□ 24-1 成長背景
□ 24-2 三個目標
□ 24-3 末日博士甦醒
□ 必考字彙大回顧

Unit 25 Quicksilver 快銀
□ 25-1 成長背景
□ 25-2 修補裂痕
□ 25-3 新的力量
□ 必考字彙大回顧

Unit 26 Magneto 萬磁王
□ 26-1 成長背景
□ 26-2 打回原形
□ 26-3 突變體家園
□ 必考字彙大回顧

Unit 27 TMNT 忍者龜
□ 27-1 成長背景
□ 27-2 多元組合
□ 27-3 完成培訓
□ 必考字彙大回顧

是否能晉升為超能字彙英雄？
★完成10小節 →「肉雞小英雄」
★完成27小節 →「小小英雄達人」
★完成36小節 →「傳奇英雄」

The Forbidden Love
禁忌的愛

During Thor's upbringing, Odin decided to send his son to earth to learn **humility**. He placed Thor into the body of Donald Blake, a **partially disabled** medical student. At that time, Thor lost his memories of **godhood**, and became a doctor in Norway. When Thor **witnessed** the arrival of an alien, he ran away, carelessly falling into a cave, where he discovered his hammer Mjolnir. He stroked it against a rock, and he transformed into the Thunder God.

Thor started his double life, spending most of his time treating the ill in a private practice, and at

在索爾的成長過程中，奧丁決定送兒子到地球去學習謙虛。他讓雷神成為一個部份殘疾的醫學系學生，唐納德・布萊克。當時，雷神失去了當神的記憶，而成為挪威的醫生。當索爾親眼目睹了一個外星人的到來。他逃跑，而不慎掉進一個山洞裡。在那裡，他發現他的錘子雷神之鎚。他將它敲向石頭，他便轉變成雷神。

索爾開始了他的雙重生活。他將大部分時間花費在私人診

the same time fighting evils to help **humanity**. During his practice, he fell in love with the nurse, Jane Foster, who is a normal human being. Thor wanted to marry Jane, but Odin **rejected** the request. Thor **disobeyed** his father and refused to return to Asgard. Odin eventually gave in and allowed Thor to date Jane Foster under the **condition** that she passes a **trial**. Foster's failing in the test made Thor understand that she is very much different from him.

所治療病人。與此同時，他打擊犯罪幫助人類。在他的工作中，他愛上了一位普通人的護士，珍‧福斯特。索爾想娶珍，但奧丁拒絕了這一個要求。索爾違背了他的父親，並拒絕返回仙宮。奧丁最終放棄，只要珍通過考驗，就允許索爾與珍在一起。福斯特未能通過試驗使索爾了解到珍‧福斯特與他是有很大區別的。

卡漫精選字彙表

單字	詞性	中譯	單字	詞性	中譯
humility	*n.*	謙卑	humanity	*n.*	人性
partially	*adv.*	部分地	reject	*v.*	拒絕
disable	*v.*	使傷殘	disobey	*v.*	不服從
godhood	*n.*	神格	condition	*n.*	情況
witness	*n.*	見證人	trial	*n.*	考驗

MP3 56

 ### *Half Brother, Forever Foe*
同父異母的兄弟，永遠的敵人

When Thor was sent to earth, it attracted the attention of his **adoptive** brother, Loki. While Thor was a kid, he was raised **alongside** Loki, who was adopted by Odin after Loki's father, Laufey got killed in a battle.

當索爾被送到地球，這引起了他的收養的弟弟洛基的注意。當索爾還是個孩子時，他與在戰鬥中喪生的洛飛的兒子，現在是奧丁的養子，洛基一起長大。

Loki had been jealous of Thor ever since they were kids. The jealousy never went away. It **gradually** increased to a point that Loki desired to kill Thor.

洛基從小就嫉妒索爾。嫉妒從來沒有消失過。它逐漸上升到洛基需要殺死索爾的程度。

Loki even tried to use illusion of the Hulk to draw Thor into battle. However, it resulted in the **formation** of the Avengers – Captain America, Iron Man, Ant Man, Hulk, Black Widow, Thor, and many

洛基甚至試圖利用浩克的錯覺逼索爾投入戰鬥。然而，這卻導致了復仇者的形成 - 美國隊長、鋼鐵人、蟻人、綠巨人、

more. Besides Loki, Thor also had several other foes including Zarrko, the Radioactive Man, the Lava Man, the Cobra and Mister Hyde.

黑寡婦、索爾等等。除了洛基以外，索爾也有其他幾個對手包括Zarrko、放射性人、熔岩人、眼鏡蛇和海德先生。

卡漫精選字彙表

單字	詞性	中譯	單字	詞性	中譯
adoptive	*adj.*	採用的	gradually	*adv.*	逐步地
alongside	*adv.*	在旁邊	formation	*n.*	形成

MP3 57

Power of Thunder God
雷力神

Like all Asgardians, Thor has **immunity** to all earthly disease, thus has **an incredibly** long life. Thor also has the strongest body of the Asgardians. He is able to push over the leaning Tower of Pisa with one finger and **rip** apart the Golden Gate Bridge.

如同所有阿斯嘉特人，索爾具有對一切塵世疾病的免疫力，因而具有令人難以置信的長壽命。索爾還具有阿斯嘉特人強壯的身體。他能用一根手指推動比薩斜塔和撕碎金門大橋。

He also has a very high resistance to injury, and he **possesses keen** senses which allow him to travel faster than light and hear noise from the other planets. Thor even has the ability to cure wounds of his body with the Mjolnir. And as the Thunder God, with his Mjolnir, Thor is able to control the **elements** and create storms.

他也對於傷害有非常高的阻力，他擁有敏銳的感官，使他能夠比光還快，還能從其他行星聽到噪音。索爾甚至有利用神斧治癒他身體創傷的能力。而作為雷神，他可以用他的神盾控制元素，並創建風暴。

He can even lift the entire building with the wind. His signature weapons are the Belt of Strength and the hammer, Mjolnir.

The Belt of Strength doubles Thor's power which makes him unbeatable, where the hammer, Mjolnir can be used not only for fights but also for controlling weather.

他甚至可以利用風舉起整幢大樓。他的招牌武器是他的力量皮帶和雷神之鎚。

力量皮帶帶給雷神兩倍的力量，這使得他無與倫比，雷神之錐不僅可用於戰鬥，也可用於控制天氣條件。

卡漫精選字彙表

單字	詞性	中譯	單字	詞性	中譯
immunity	*n.*	免疫性	possess	*v.*	擁有
incredibly	*adv.*	難以置信地	keen	*adj.*	敏銳的
rip	*v.*	撕	element	*n.*	元素

01　劃時代的傳奇

02　不朽的英雄神話

03　無堅不摧背後的英雄血淚

04　永存於人們心中的英雄霸主

必考字彙大回顧

卡漫超給力字彙表

單字	中譯	詞性	反義字	反義字中譯
cave	洞穴	n.		
humility	謙卑	n.	arrogance	傲慢
partially	部分地	adv.	completely	全然地
disable	使傷殘	v.		
godhood	神格	n.	devil	魔鬼
witness	見證人	n.	participant	參加者
humanity	人性	n.		
reject	拒絕	v.	accept	接受
disobey	不服從	v.	obey	遵守
condition	情況	n.		
trial	考驗	n.		
foe	敵人	n.	ally	盟友
adoptive	採用的	adj.		
alongside	在旁邊	adv.	away	遙遠
gradually	逐步地	adv.	rapidly	急速地
formation	形成	n.	destruction	毀壞
immunity	免疫性	n.		
incredible	難以置信的	adj.	believable	可信的
rip	撕	v.	mend	修補
possess	擁有	v.	lack	缺乏
keen	敏銳的	adj.	dull	遲鈍的
element	元素	n.		

Sorcery Instead of Strength
巫術而不是超能力

Even though Loki grew up with the Asgardians, his body actually **flowed** with the Frost Giants' blood. The Asgardians and the Frost Giants are **ancient** enemies. After the battle with Loki's father, Laufey, Odin found a baby. Odin raised Loki alongside his **biological** son, Thor.

Since childhood, Loki knew he was different from other Asgardians. For example, the Asgardians valued great strength, **tenacity**, and **bravery** in battles, which Loki was not good at and was **inferior** to. On the other hand, Loki was gifted with sorcery and magic. He was considered to be one of the best **wizards** within Asgardians, secretly wishing he could use his power to become the

即使洛基與阿斯嘉特人一同成長，他的身體畢竟流著冰霜巨人的血液。在與洛基的父親戰鬥後，奧丁發現了一個嬰兒。奧丁一起扶養洛基與他的親生兒子雷神索爾。

自從孩童時期，洛基知道自己跟其他阿思嘉特人不同。例如，阿斯嘉特人在對戰時巨大的力量、堅韌和勇敢被認為是偉大的特質，在這些技能洛基並不如阿斯嘉特人。在另一方面，洛基具有巫術和魔法的天賦。他被視為阿

most powerful god and destroy Thor. He had earned a nickname as the God of **Mischief**. because he enjoys playing **pranks** on people around him. But things got worse and worse as his power grew more **malicious**. He earned another nicknamed the God of Evil.

斯嘉特人中最好的巫師，他暗暗希望他可以利用自己的能力，成為最強大的神並摧毀索爾。因此，他贏得了一個惡作劇之神的綽號，因為他給周圍的人惡作劇。但是當他長大力量變得更加險惡，事情也變得越來越糟糕。他獲得了另一個綽號邪惡的神。

卡漫精選字彙表

單字	詞性	中譯	單字	詞性	中譯
flow	v.	流動	bravery	n.	勇敢
ancient	adj.	古代的	inferior	adj.	低等的
shame	v.	羞愧	wizard	n.	男巫
biological	adj.	生物的	prank	n.	惡作劇
sorcery	n.	巫術	mischief	n.	惡作劇
tenacity	n.	固執	malicious	adj.	惡意的

MP3 58

 Hate Each Other Yet Sometimes Work as a Team
討厭對方然而有時卻為一個團隊

Loki set up his goal a long time ago – to destroy Thor and **seize** Asgard. Odin couldn't stand Loki's behavior and once magically **imprisoned** Loki within a tree. As the greatest wizard, Loki freed himself from his prison and became more **consumed** than ever before. Everything he did and everything he planned was to take down Thor.

He sometimes **confronted** Thor directly, and sometimes used various **pawns** to achieve his goal. Loki even tried to turn Odin against his own son and steal the magical hammer, Mjolnir. None of his plan succeeds though. He then tried to manipulate the Hulk to kill Thor,

洛基在很久以前便設立了自己的目標 - 摧毀雷神和掌權仙宮。奧丁對洛基的行為看不下去，因此曾經利用魔法將洛基囚禁在樹中。作為最偉大的巫師，洛基逃脫監獄，並比以前更變本加厲。他所做的任何事與他所計畫的一切都是要打倒雷神。

他有時直接面對雷神，有時使用各種棋子來實現他的目標。洛基甚至試圖使奧丁與自己的兒子反目，並偷走神奇之鎚，雷神之鎚。雖然，他的計劃都沒有

which accidentally led Thor to form the Avengers.

Regardless of the fact that Loki hated Thor and tried whatever he could to destroy him, when there were enemies trying to **defeat** Asgard, Loki partnered with Odin and Thor to **defend** them. It is because Loki wants to become the leader of Asgard, he will not allow anyone to destroy the paradise he wants to rule.

成功。然後，他試圖操縱浩克來殺死索爾時，意外導致索爾成為復仇者。

無論洛基多恨索爾，並試圖不顧一切的消滅他，但當有敵人試圖打敗阿斯嘉特時，洛基與奧丁和索爾合作攻防。這是因為洛基想成為阿斯嘉特的領導人，他不會允許任何人破壞他想統治的天堂。

卡漫精選字彙表

單字	詞性	中譯	單字	詞性	中譯
seize	*v.*	捉住	pawn	*v.*	抵押
imprison	*v.*	監禁	defeat	*v.*	擊敗
consume	*v.*	花費	defend	*v.*	保護
confront	*v.*	面臨			

01 劃時代的傳奇

02 不朽的英雄神話

03 無堅不摧背後的英雄血淚

04 永存於人們心中的英雄霸主

MP3 58

Wizard Power
巫師的能力

As a wizard, Loki does not use weapons that normal Asgardians use.

作為一個巫師，洛基不使用阿斯嘉特人一般所使用的武器。

Instead, he uses magical power objects, such as the Norn Stones or rare Asgardian herbs.

反之，他利用具有魔術功能的物體，如諾恩石頭或阿斯嘉特的稀有藥材。

The potions he creates help him enhance his **immediate** personal strength and creates **permanent** transformations.

他所創造的魔藥可以幫助他增強他眼前的個人實力，創造永久的轉變。

As a prank, he once transformed Thor into a frog while Thor was on earth.

作為一個惡作劇之人，他曾經將在地球的索爾變為一個青蛙。

Thor returned to his normal

索爾之後利用洛

form later on by Loki's sword.

基的劍變回他正常的
樣貌。

卡漫精選字彙表

單字	詞性	中譯	單字	詞性	中譯
immediate	*adj.*	即刻的	**permanent**	*adj.*	永久的

必考字彙大回顧

卡漫超給力字彙表

單字	中譯	詞性	反義字	反義字中譯
flow	流動	*v.*	cease	停止
ancient	古代的	*adj.*	current	當前的
shame	羞愧	*v.*	honor	榮譽
biological	生物的	*adj.*		
sorcery	巫術	*n.*	reality	現實
tenacity	固執	*n.*	easy going	隨和的
bravery	勇敢	*n.*	cowardice	怯懦
inferior	低等的	*adj.*	superior	優越的
wizard	男巫	*n.*	witch	女巫
prank	惡作劇	*n.*		
mischief	惡作劇	*n.*		
malicious	惡意的	*adj.*	pleasant	愉快的
seize	捉住	*v.*	lose	失去
imprison	監禁	*v.*	liberate	解放
consume	花費	*v.*	conserve	養護
confront	面臨	*v.*	evade	逃避
pawn	抵押	*v.*	redeem	贖回
defeat	擊敗	*v.*	lose	失去
defend	保護	*v.*	attack	攻擊
immediate	即刻的	*adj.*	eventual	最終的
permanent	永久的	*adj.*	temporary	臨時的

The Very First Human Green Lantern
第一位綠光戰警

The Green **Lanterns** are a group of superheroes who were selected to guard the **universe**. There are over 3600 Green Lanterns and not all of them are human beings. They are all **monitored** and **empowered** by **mystical creatures** called the Guardians. The very first Green Lantern is a railroad engineer named Alan Scott. Once when he was on a business trip, he was in a railway crash. Luckily, he wasn't killed.

As the only survivor, he found himself holding a magic lantern which spoke to him and guided him to craft the bottom part of the lantern into a ring. The ring gave him a wide **variety** of powers. He

綠光戰警是一組被挑選來守護宇宙的超級英雄。有超過3600位綠光戰警，但不是所有人都是人類。他們都被稱為監護人的生物監測及賦予力量。第一位綠光戰警是一個名為艾倫·斯科特的鐵路工程師。有一次，在他出差時，他在鐵路出車禍。幸運的是，他並沒有死亡。

作為唯一的倖存者，他發現自己拿著的幻燈對他說話，引導他將燈籠的底座運用手工藝做成一枚戒指。這個戒指給了他

basically could control anything as long as he concentrated on his thought with the ring on.

Although, the ring needed to be charged every 24 hours by touching it to the lantern for a time. He then created a superhero costume and became a crime fighter. Alan used his power to fight villains and kept the earth a safe place.

各種各樣的能力。只要他專注在戒指上，他基本上就能控制任何事物。

雖然這枚戒指每24小時就需要觸碰燈籠來充電。他後來創造了一個超級英雄的服裝，開始打擊犯罪。艾倫用自己的力量對抗惡棍和保持地球的安全。

卡漫精選字彙表

單字	詞性	中譯	單字	詞性	中譯
lantern	*n.*	燈籠	mystical	*adj.*	神祕的
universe	*n.*	宇宙	creature	*n.*	生物
monitor	*v.*	監控	variety	*n.*	多樣化
empower	*v.*	授權			

MP3 62

The Most Well-Known Green Lantern
最知名的綠光戰警

The most well-known green lantern must be Halrold Jordan, A.K.A "Hal" Jordan. One day after his practice, he found a dying alien named Abin Sur.

最知名的綠光戰警是哈洛德・喬丹，又名「哈爾」喬丹。有一天在他下班後，他發現一個名為阿斌蘇爾的垂死外星人。

He gave the power ring and lantern to Hal. Hal then became the **galactic** police and a member of the Green Lantern Corps. His job is to protect all life in Sector 2814. One of his **trainers** was his mentor, Sinestro, who was also one of the best Green Lanterns. During his training, he once found out that Sinestro has been **subjugating** the earth. Hal reported the act to the Guardians and he fought Sinestro and **emerged** victorious. Sinestro later on was **expelled** from the

他將能力戒指和燈籠給了哈爾。哈爾隨後成為了銀河警察和綠光戰警軍團的一員。他的工作是保護2184部門的所有生物。他的教練也是他的心靈導師，賽尼斯托，也是最好的綠光戰警之一。在他受訓時，他有一次發現賽尼斯托已經開始征服地球。哈爾向監護人報告了這件事，與賽

Corps and became an enemy to the Corps.

Hal is also a ladies' man. You can always find beautiful women around him, but the one to whom Hal may be closest to was Carol Ferris, his boss at Ferris Aircraft. The relationship didn't last though, because of Carol's **dedication** to running her company, and also she was chosen by the Zamarons be to Star Sapphire, who is a powerful super-**villainess**.

尼斯托交手並取得了勝利。賽尼斯托後來被部隊開除,並成為一個敵人軍團。

哈爾也是個被女人寵愛的男人。你總是可以在他身邊找到漂亮的女人,但與哈爾最接近的人可能是卡羅·費里斯,他在費里斯飛機的老闆。雖然這段關係並沒有持續,因為卡羅為她的公司奉獻,而且還被札馬倫選擇成為星光藍寶石,一個能力強大的超級壞女人。

01 劃時代的傳奇

02 不朽的英雄神話

03 無堅不摧背後的英雄血淚

04 永存於人們心中的英雄霸主

卡漫精選字彙表

單字	詞性	中譯	單字	詞性	中譯
seek	*v.*	尋找	emerge	*v.*	浮現
galactic	*adj.*	銀河的	expel	*v.*	驅逐
trainer	*n.*	教練	dedication	*n.*	奉獻
subjugate	*v.*	征服	villainess	*n.*	女反派角色

MP3 63 ▶

The Yellow Impurity
黃色雜質

There was a time that Hal somehow went crazy and destroyed the Lantern Corp and the Central Power Battery.

曾經有一段時間哈爾莫名其妙地瘋了，摧毀了燈籠和中央動力電池。

For years he went to the dark side and called himself Parallex. Parallex was the yellow **impurity** which represented the physical **embodiment** of fear on the **emotional electromagnetic spectrum**.

多年來，他走到黑暗的一面，並自稱「視差」。「視差」是代表恐懼的情緒，電磁頻譜物理現象的黃色雜質。

The total opposite of the green **willpower.** Indeed, is one of the greatest secrets kept by the Guardians.

與代表意志力的綠色完全相反。事實上，這是監護人最大的秘密之一。

It was not until the Sun was threatened by the Sun-Eater did Hal overcome his fear, sacrifice himself, and **expend** the last of his

但直到太陽被太陽食者威脅，哈爾才克服自己的恐懼，犧牲了自己，並花費他

vast power to **reignite** the Sun.

最後的巨大力量重新
點燃太陽。

卡漫精選字彙表

單字	詞性	中譯	單字	詞性	中譯
impurity	*n.*	雜質	**spectrum**	*n.*	光譜
embodiment	*n.*	具體化	**willpower**	*n.*	意志力
emotional	*adj.*	易動情的	**expend**	*v.*	耗費
electromagnetic	*adj.*	電磁的	**reignite**	*v.*	再點燃

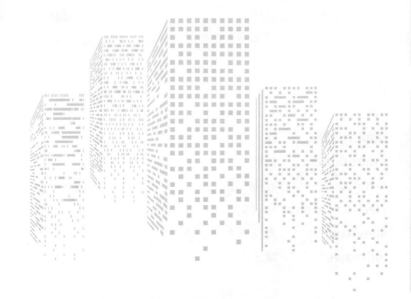

必考字彙大回顧

卡漫超給力字彙表

單字	中譯	詞性	反義字	反義字中譯
lantern	燈籠	*n.*		
universe	宇宙	*n.*		
monitor	監控	*v.*	ignore	忽視
empower	授權	*v.*	forbid	禁止
mystical	神祕的	*adj.*		
creature	生物	*n.*		
variety	多樣化	*n.*	similarity	相似
seek	尋找	*v.*		
galactic	銀河的	*adj.*		
trainer	教練	*n.*	pupil	弟子
subjugate	征服	*v.*	surrender	投降
emerge	浮現	*v.*	disappear	消失
expel	驅逐	*v.*	hire	錄用
dedication	奉獻	*n.*		
villainess	女反派角色	*n.*		
impurity	雜質	*n.*	purity	純度
embodiment	具體化	*n.*		
emotional	易動情的	*adj.*	impassive	冷漠的
electromagnetic	電磁的	*adj.*		
spectrum	光譜	*n.*		
willpower	意志力	*n.*		

單字	中譯	詞性	反義字	反義字中譯
expend	耗費	*v.*	**accumulate**	積累
reignite	再點燃	*v.*		

01
劃時代的傳奇

02
不朽的英雄神話

03
無堅不摧背後的英雄血淚

04
永存於人們心中的英雄霸主

MP3 63

 The Secret of Sinestro
賽尼斯托的秘密

How come the famous Har Jordan's mentor became Green Lanters' most **enduring** enemy? Let's find out. Sinestro was born on the planet Korugar in sector 1417. He was working as an **anthropologist** and specializing in **reconstructions** of ruins of long-dead **civilizations.**

Just like Har Jordan, one day, an alien named Prohl Gosgotha crashed the spaceship and was found by Sinestro. Prohl was badly injured and dying. Once he saw Sinestro, he quickly explained who he was and gave him the ring. Sinestro barely knew what was going on, but was already chased by the **pursuer** from Qward.

為什麼著名的哈爾‧喬丹的恩師會成為綠光戰警最長久的敵人？讓我們來了解一下。賽尼斯特出生在1417部門，克路加星球上。他的工作是一位人類學家，並專精於重建早已摧毀的文明遺址。

就如同哈爾‧喬丹，有一天，一個名為普羅‧加斯加挈的外星人的太空船墜毀，並且被賽尼斯托找到。普羅受重傷，近乎死亡。他一看見了賽尼斯托，就連忙解釋他是誰並給賽尼斯托他的戒指。賽尼

斯特幾乎不知道發生了什麼事情，但當時已被科瓦德的追趕者們追殺。

He took the ring and ran away. Later on, Prohl turned out to be still alive and asked for his ring back. Sinestro decided not to give Prohl the ring back and left him for dead. This secret was never revealed.

他拿著戒指就跑了。後來，普羅原來還活著，並想要回他的戒指。賽尼斯托決定不將戒指還給普羅，並讓他死亡。這個秘密一直沒有被揭露出來。

卡漫精選字彙表

單字	詞性	中譯	單字	詞性	中譯
enduring	*adj.*	耐久的	civilization	*n.*	文明
anthropologist	*n.*	人類學家	pursuer	*n.*	追趕者
reconstruction	*n.*	重建			

Decision to Rule the Universe
統治宇宙的決定

His ambition led him not only to protect his **sector**, but also to **preserve** orders in the society of his home planet regardless of the cost. Eventually, he decided he was going to conquer Korugar and rule the Universe. Sinestro was **assigned** to be Hal Jordan's instructor when Hal first joined the Green Lantern Corps. Sinestro was a very strict instructor. He used the **totalitarian** method and believed his **iron-fisted** rule was necessary to protect his people from alien forces. During their training, Hal helped Sinestro **repel** an attempted **invasion** of Korugar by the alien **warlords** known as the Khunds.

When Jordan called for help,

他的野心使他不僅要保護他的部門，而且也不計成本地保護他出生的行星。最終，他決定要去征服克路加和統治宇宙。賽尼斯托被分配到當哈爾·喬丹的教練時，哈爾首次加入綠色戰警。賽尼斯特是一個非常嚴格的教練。他用極權主義的方法，並相信他的鐵腕統治是必要的，以保護他的人民及外來勢力。培訓期間，哈爾幫助賽尼斯托擊退入侵的被稱為寬德的外星人軍。

當喬丹大聲呼

Sinestro's secret was revealed. He was later forced to appear before the Guardians for punishment. The Guardians **banished** Sinestro to the **antimatter** universe which was made up of negative matters. He started to hate the Guardians as much as the Weaponers do. The Weaponers **convinced** Sinestro to ally with them and offered to help Sinestro gain revenge on the Guardians.

救，賽尼斯托的秘密被揭露。後來他被監護人逼迫出庭並進行處罰。監護人放逐賽尼斯托到充滿負面能量的反物質星球。他開始與戰士一樣痛恨監護人。戰士説服了賽尼斯托與他們結盟，並表示願意幫助賽尼斯托對守護者復仇。

卡漫精選字彙表

單字	詞性	中譯	單字	詞性	中譯
sector	*n.*	扇形	repel	*v.*	擊退
preserve	*v.*	保留	invasion	*n.*	侵入
assign	*v.*	分配	banish	*v.*	放逐
totalitarian	*n.*	極權主義	antimatter	*n.*	反物質
iron-fisted	*prep.*	鐵腕	convince	*v.*	説服

MP3 66

The Devil that Never Dies
永不熄滅的魔鬼

The Weaponers also created a yellow power ring for Sinestro to use which made him the most powerful enemy of the Green Lanterns because the power of Green Lanterns will be affected by the Yellow Ring.

戰士還做了一個黃色能源戒指給賽尼斯托使用，這個使得賽尼斯托成為綠光戰警最強大的敵人，因為綠光戰警的能力會因為黃色戒指而受影響。

Even so, Hal still found his way to defeat him. During a battle, Hal tricked Sinestro and imprisoned him in a green bubble. Sinestro did find his way to escape, but again was caught. The Guardians kept him imprisoned and **constructed** an **inescapable** prison for Sinestro before the Guardians took a leave of **absence** from their universe.

即便如此，哈爾仍然發現他的方式以擊敗賽尼斯托。在一場戰役中，哈爾騙過賽尼斯托，將他監禁在一個綠色泡泡之中。賽尼斯托找到他的方式逃脫，但再次被捕。當守護者需要離開自己的宇宙時，守護者將他囚禁在一個無法逃脫的監獄

Sinestro was so smart and managed to free himself by manipulating the Mad God of Sector 3600. He killed the entire star systems, but was finally **vanquished** by the Green Lanterns. He was **condemned** to death, but again Sinestro managed to send his **essence** into the Central Power Battery which we know as Parallax to create an illusion (the Yellow Impurity) that made people believe he was dead.

賽尼斯托是如此的聰明，他有辦法操縱管理3600區域的瘋神，並釋放他自己。他破壞了整個恆星系統，但最終被綠光戰警征服。他被判處死刑，但同樣的賽尼斯托設法將他的精髓送入中央電池，創造出我們所知道的「視差」來欺騙死亡—也就是黃色雜質。

卡漫精選字彙表

單字	詞性	中譯	單字	詞性	中譯
prevent	*v.*	避免	vanquish	*v.*	征服
construct	*v.*	構造	condemn	*v.*	譴責
inescapable	*adj.*	不可避免的	essence	*n.*	本質
absence	*n.*	缺席			

必考字彙大回顧

卡漫超給力字彙表

單字	中譯	詞性	反義字	反義字中譯
enduring	耐久的	*adj.*	short-lived	短命的
anthropologist	人類學家	*n.*		
reconstruction	重建	*n.*	neglect	忽略
civilization	文明	*n.*		
pursuer	追趕者	*n.*		
sector	扇形	*n.*		
preserve	保留	*v.*	destroy	破壞
assign	分配	*v.*	retain	保留
totalitarian	極權主義	*n.*	democratic	民主
iron-fisted	鐵腕	*prep.*	easy-going	隨和
repel	擊退	*v.*	attract	吸引
invasion	侵入	*n.*	obedience	服從
banish	放逐	*v.*	keep	保持
antimatter	反物質	*n.*		
convince	說服	*v.*	discourage	不鼓勵
prevent	避免	*v.*	encourage	鼓勵
construct	構造	*v.*	demolish	拆除
inescapable	不可避免的	*adj.*	escapable	可逃避的
absence	缺席	*n.*	presence	存在
vanquish	征服	*v.*	fail	失敗
condemn	譴責	*v.*	commend	表彰
essence	本質	*n.*	exterior	外觀

The Excellent Student from a Bad Neighborhood
惡劣環境中的優秀學生

Benjamin Jacob Grimm was born on Yancy Street, a tough neighborhood in the Lower East Side of New York City. Due to a family tragedy, Ben was raised by his uncle Jake. Ben found a way to survive in the neighborhood and once led the Yancy Street gang. Even though he was raised in a bad area, he did very well in football in high school. Thus, he received a full scholarship to Empire State University.

班傑明・雅各・格林出生於紐約下東城附近很難生存的楊希街。由於家庭悲劇，班是由他的叔叔傑克所帶大的。班發現他在鄰里中生存的方式，曾經一度領導楊希街的幫派。雖然他是在一個壞區長大，他在高中時的足球成績很好，因此，他獲得了全額獎學金進入了帝國州立大學。

He met his **lifelong** friend, Reed Richards, who was **basically** a genius. When they were in school, Reed often told Ben that his dream was to build a space rocket to

他遇到了他一生的朋友，一位天才，里德・李查茲。當他們在學校時，里德經常告訴班，他的夢想

explore the **regions** of space around Mars.

After earning his degree in engineering, Ben joined the United States **Marine** Corps and became a test pilot. Later on, he joined the Air Force. He was ordered to serve as a pilot during a top secret **surveillance** mission into Vladivostok in the Soviet Union. His partners were Logan, who became Wolverine, and Carol Danvers, who became Ms. Marvel in the future. After that, he became an **astronaut** for NASA.

是建立一個太空火箭，探索火星周圍的空間區域。

得到他的工程學位後，班加入了美國海軍陸戰隊，成為一名試飛員。後來，他加入了空軍。他奉命在蘇聯符拉迪沃斯托克的秘密任務中作為飛行員。他的合作夥伴是洛根，最終成為金剛狼，和卡羅·丹佛斯，未來成為驚奇女士。在此之後，他成為了美國宇航局的宇航員。

卡漫精選字彙表

單字	詞性	中譯	單字	詞性	中譯
scholarship	n.	獎學金	region	n.	地區
lifelong	prep.	終身	marine	n.	海洋
basically	adv.	基本上	surveillance	n.	監控
explore	v.	探索	astronaut	n.	太空人

01 劃時代的傳奇

02 不朽的英雄神話

03 無堅不摧背後的英雄血淚

04 永存於人們心中的英雄霸主

Radiation Caused the Birth of the Thing
輻射造成石頭人的誕生

Years later, Reed actually built the spaceship. However, the government **denied** his **permission** to fly the spaceship by himself. Therefore, he contacted Ben and asked Ben to fly with him in secret. Ben was **reluctant** to fly the spaceship, but eventually gave in.

Reed, his wife Susan Storm, her brother Johnny Storm and Ben took the **unauthorized** ride into the upper **atmosphere** of Earth and the Van Allen Belts. Right at that moment, their spaceship was **pelted** by a cosmic ray storm and exposed to radiation. The spaceship crashed down to Earth. Luckily, no one was killed. Instead, all four of them found out that they

多年以後，里德竟然建成了太空船。然而，政府否決了他自己飛行太空船的許可。因此，他聯繫班，並要求班與他秘密飛行。班原本是不願飛太空船的，但最終同意。

里德和他的妻子蘇珊史東，她的弟弟強尼史東和班擅自開往大氣層上層的艾倫輻射帶。就在那一刻，他們的太空飛船被宇宙射線風暴攻擊並暴露在輻射中。飛船墜毀。幸運的是，沒有人死亡。反而，他們四個發現，他們

had gained superhuman powers.

Ben's skin got transformed into a thick, **lumpy** orange hide. He became The Thing. Ben was unhappy with his transformation, but still decided to use his super power to help humanity. He did try many ways to transform back to his human form, but his body rejected all the **attempts**. He eventually accepted the fact that he will forever be The Thing.

都獲得了超能力。

班的皮膚變成厚厚的、詭異的橙色皮。他變成石頭人。班不滿他的轉變，但還是決定用自己的超能力幫助人類。他也嘗試了很多方法來改造回到他的人形，但他的身體拒絕了所有的嘗試。他最終接受了這個事實，他將永遠成為石頭人。

卡漫精選字彙表

單字	詞性	中譯	單字	詞性	中譯
deny	*v.*	拒絕	atmosphere	*n.*	大氣層
permission	*n.*	允許	pelt	*n.*	毛皮
reluctant	*v.*	不情願	lumpy	*adj.*	凹凸不平的
unauthorized	*adj.*	擅自	attempt	*v.*	嘗試

01 劃時代的傳奇

02 不朽的英雄神話

03 無堅不摧背後的英雄血淚

04 永存於人們心中的英雄霸主

MP3 69

Lumpy Skin, Giant Body, Nimble Mind and Skill
凹凸不平的皮膚，巨大的身軀，靈活的頭腦和技巧

As his body is covered with an orange, **flexible**, rock-like skin, the Thing is capable of surviving impacts of great strength and force.

由於他的身體上覆蓋著一層橙色的、靈活的、岩石般的皮膚，石頭人能夠承受強大力量與壓力。

He can also **withstand** gunfire. He does get injured and he does bleed, but you can never **seriously** hurt him.

他也能承受槍炮。他會受傷也會流血，但你永遠無法嚴重傷害他。

Not only **externally**, the Thing's senses can withstand higher levels of **sensory stimulation** than a regular human being, except the sense of touch due to his thick skin.

不僅在外部，石頭人的厚皮可以感受到比一般人更纖細的感官刺激，除了觸覺以外。

And even though he only has three fingers and a thumb on each hand after transforming in to the Thing, his actions are not affected

即使他左右各只有三根手指和一個拇指，他的行動並不會受到一點影響。他仍

by this a bit. He remains a great fighter and a skilled pilot.

然是一個偉大的戰士和一個熟練的飛行員。

卡漫精選字彙表

單字	詞性	中譯	單字	詞性	中譯
flexible	*adj.*	靈活	externally	*adv.*	外部
withstand	*v.*	經得起	sensory	*adj.*	感覺的
seriously	*adv.*	認真地	stimulation	*n.*	促進

必考字彙大回顧

卡漫超給力字彙表

單字	中譯	詞性	反義字	反義字中譯
scholarship	獎學金	*n.*		
lifelong	終身	*prep.*	temporary	纖細
basically	基本上	*adv.*	additionally	附加地
explore	探索	*v.*	overlook	忽略
region	地區	*n.*		
marine	海洋	*n.*		
surveillance	監控	*n.*	negligence	疏忽
astronaut	太空人	*n.*		
deny	拒絕	*v.*	agree	同意
permission	允許	*n.*	denial	否認
reluctant	不情願	*v.*	willing	願意
unauthorized	擅自	*adj.*	authorized	經批准的
atmosphere	大氣層	*n.*		
pelt	毛皮	*n.*		
lumpy	凹凸不平的	*adj.*	smooth	光滑的
attempt	嘗試	*v.*	retreat	撤退
nimble	敏捷	*adj.*	stiff	僵硬
flexible	靈活	*adj.*	inflexible	剛硬的
withstand	經得起	*v.*		
seriously	認真地	*adv.*	jokingly	開玩笑地
externally	外部	*adv.*	internally	內部

單字	中譯	詞性	反義字	反義字中譯
sensory	感覺的	*adj.*	**intellectual**	理智的
stimulation	促進	*n.*	**discouragement**	勸阻

Rivalry Instead of Friendship
競爭而非友誼

Victor is not so much an enemy of the Thing as the enemy of the **Fantastic** Four. Victor von Doom was born in a small European country named Latveria. His parents are Werner, a doctor and Cynthia von Doom, a witch who had **invoked** the **demon** Mephisto for power. His parents died when he was young, leaving him to Werner's best friend, Boris, to take care of Victor.

When Victor found out about his mother's **mystical artifacts**, he started to learn **sorcery** by himself, hoping to set his mother's soul

與其說維克多是石頭人的一個敵人，可能更適合說，他是驚奇4超人的敵人。維克多‧馮‧杜姆出生在一個名為拉托維尼亞的小小歐洲國家。他的父母是沃納（一名醫生）和辛西婭‧馮‧杜姆（一個向惡魔墨菲斯托請求能力的巫婆）。他父母於他年輕時就過世，把他留給沃納最好的朋友鮑里斯來照顧維克多。

當維克多發現了他母親的神秘文物，他開始自己學習巫術，希望可以解放他

free. After graduating from elementary school, he became a scientific genius. His works were somehow seen by the American Academies. He was invited to the New York's Empire State University on a full scholarship.

After checking himself into the university, Victor was **assigned** to the same room as Reed Richards, but somehow Victor just didn't like the **arrangement**. He refused to share a room with Reed and rejected to be friends with him. **Throughout** his university days, Victor **pursed** a rivalry with Reed.

母親的靈魂。小學畢業後，他成為了一個科學天才。他的作品在某種程度上被美國科學院看到。他被邀請以全額獎學金的方式到紐約帝國州立大學就讀。

報到入學後，維克多被分配到與里德‧李查茲同一個房間，但不知為何維克多就是不喜歡這個安排。他拒絕與里德分一個房間，並拒絕與他交朋友。在他的大學時代，維克多多次與里德較勁。

01 劃時代的傳奇

02 不朽的英雄神話

03 無堅不摧背後的英雄血淚

04 永存於人們心中的英雄霸主

卡漫精選字彙表

單字	詞性	中譯	單字	詞性	中譯
fantastic	adj.	極好的	rivalry	n.	對抗
invoke	n.	調用	assign	v.	分配
demon	n.	惡魔	arrangement	n.	安排
mystical	adj.	神秘的	throughout	prep.	始終
artifact	n.	神器			

MP3 71

 The New Leader of Latveria
拉脫維尼亞的新領導人

To rescue his mother's soul from the **netherworld**, he spent a lot of time inventing a machine, but miscalculation in his work not only caused a huge explosion, but also ruined his appearance and get him expelled from school.

He decided to leave the States and went to Tibet to seek new **enlightenment**. He found the Aged Genghis and a long-lost order of monks. The monks made the first suit of armor which hid his **features** from the world. The mask was also put on him before it was cooled.

Victor went back to his homeland Latveria, using his **genius** and technology to transform it into

為了從陰間拯救他媽媽的靈魂，他花許多時間發明機器。但是計算失誤不只導致巨大的爆炸，更使得他毀容跟遭學校開除。

他決定離開美國，去西藏尋求新的啟示。他發現了老年的成吉思汗和久違的僧侶。僧侶們做第一套兵器，讓他可以在世界中隱藏他的真實身份。面具也在冷卻前被戴上。

維克多又回到了他的祖國拉托維尼亞，用他的天才和技

the Doom Utopia. Victor set up three goals: to rescue his mother's soul, to be better than Reed Richards, and to conquer the world. Dr. Doom began an **alliance** with several different villains, such as the Sub-Mariner and alien Ovoids to gain new powers and to take down the Fantastic Four, but he was always so close to success.

術，將拉脫維尼亞改造為杜姆式的烏托邦。維克多設立了三個目標：拯救他母親的靈魂，比里德·李查茲出色，征服世界。末日博士則與幾個不同的惡棍結盟，如潛水俠和外來卵形體以獲得新的力量來打倒驚奇4超人，但他卻總是那麼接近成功。

卡漫精選字彙表

單字	詞性	中譯	單字	詞性	中譯
netherworld	*n.*	陰間	feature	*n.*	特徵
ruin	*v.*	毀壞	genius	*n.*	天才
expel	*v.*	驅逐	alliance	*n.*	聯盟
enlightenment	*n.*	啟示			

Furious and Swore to Come Back
大怒，並發誓要回來

Dr. Doom never gave up. He then engaged Reed in a mental battle at the Latverian Embassy.

末日博士從來沒有放棄過。爾後，他在拉托維尼亞大使館裡與里德開始了一場腦力的戰鬥。

Doom used an encephalo-gun and thought he had **casted** Reed into Limbo.

末日博士使用 encephalo槍，以為他已經成功地將里德推向地獄邊境。

However, in reality, Reed had **hypnotized** Doom instead. When Doom came back from the **mesmerism**, he again attacked the Fantastic Four.

然而，在現實中，里德卻催眠了末日博士。當末日博士從催眠中醒來後，他再次攻擊驚奇4超人。

The Thing was furious and crushed Doom's hands inside his **gauntlets** and allowed him to **slink**

石頭人大怒，粉碎了末日博士在手套內的手，但允許他偷

away.

Doom would never forget the **humiliation** and swore he would come back for revenge.

偷溜走。

末日博士永遠也不會忘記這個屈辱，發誓他會回來報仇。

卡漫精選字彙表

單字	詞性	中譯	單字	詞性	中譯
hypnotize	*v.*	催眠	slink	*v.*	潛逃
mesmerism	*n.*	催眠術	humiliation	*n.*	屈辱
gauntlet	*n.*	長手套			

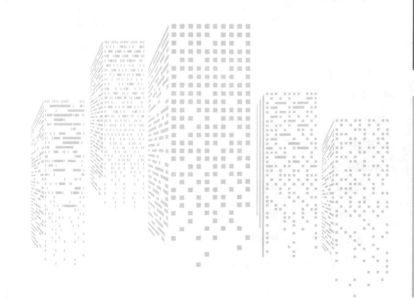

必考字彙大回顧

卡漫超給力字彙表

單字	中譯	詞性	反義字	反義字中譯
fantastic	極好的	*adj.*	awful	可怕的
invoke	調用	*n.*		
demon	惡魔	*n.*	angel	天使
mystical	神秘的	*adj.*		
artifact	神器	*n.*		
rivalry	對抗	*n.*	cooperation	合作
assign	分配	*v.*	retain	保留
arrangement	安排	*n.*	disorder	無秩序
throughout	始終	*prep.*		
netherworld	陰間	*n.*		
ruin	毀壞	*v.*	mend	
expel	驅逐	*v.*	permit	允許
enlightenment	啟示	*n.*	puzzlement	困惑
feature	特徵	*n.*		
genius	天才	*n.*	stupidity	愚蠢
dominate	支配	*v.*	follow	跟隨
mystery	神秘	*n.*		
alliance	聯盟	*n.*	antagonism	對抗
hypnotize	催眠	*v.*		
mesmerism	催眠術	*n.*		
gauntlet	長手套	*n.*		

單字	中譯	詞性	反義字	反義字中譯
slink	潛逃	*v.*		
humiliation	屈辱	*n.*	**dignity**	尊嚴

Unit 25
Quicksilver 快銀

25-1　成長背景

The Gypsy Twins
吉普賽雙胞胎

A gypsy couple, Django and Marya Miximoff have a twin brother and sister named Pietro and Wanda. Both of them **discovered** that they had **peculiar** talents when they were teenagers. One day, their gypsy camp was attacked by **villagers**.

一對吉普賽夫婦，狄亞哥和瑪麗亞梅西摩夫有對孿生兄妹名為琵也達和萬達。他們在青少年時就發現了他們有特殊的才能。有一天，他們的吉普賽營地遭到村民襲擊。

Pietro used his **phenomenal** speed and fled from the camp with his sister. Wanda and Pietro had nowhere to go. They wandered central Europe and living off the land.

琵也達用他驚人的速度與他的妹妹從營中逃出。萬達和琵也達無處可去。他們漫步歐洲中部，靠土地為生。

One day, Wanda accidentally used her **uncontrollable hex** powers and set a house on fire. They were chased away by the townspeople.

有一天，無意中萬達用了她不可控制的魔法力量，引發房子著火。他們被市民

Right before they were about to get caught, they were rescued by Magneto who is their biological father. This secret was never revealed until they were both grown up.

追逐。

在他們即將陷入對方手裡之前,他們被自己的親生父親萬磁王救出。這個秘密從未被揭露,直到他們長大。

卡漫精選字彙表

單字	詞性	中譯	單字	詞性	中譯
discover	*v.*	發現	phenomenal	*adj.*	傑出的
peculiar	*adj.*	罕見的	uncontrollable	*adj.*	不可控制的
villager	*n.*	村民	hex	*v.*	施魔法

01 劃時代的傳奇

02 不朽的英雄神話

03 無堅不摧背後的英雄血淚

04 永存於人們心中的英雄霸主

MP3 74

From Gangster to Superhero Team
從幫派到超級英雄

Magneto isn't a good **fellow** either. He owns the **Brotherhood** of Evil Mutants and made the twins become members of it as Quicksilver and the Scarlet Witch. For months they served in the Brotherhood until the **extraterrestrial** Stranger transported Magneto from earth.

They left the Brotherhood right away and joined the Avengers to become part of the hero team **alongside** Captain America and Hawkeye. Wanda had been close to her brother until she started to date the Vision.

Pietro did not agree with the relationship because the Vision is

萬磁王也不是一個好人。他擁有邪惡的突變兄弟會，並將這對雙胞胎變為其中成員，將他們命名為快銀與猩紅巫婆。幾個月來，他們兄妹都在為兄弟會服務，直到萬磁王被陌生人從地球上帶走。

他們離開了兄弟會並馬上加入了復仇者，成為英雄隊，並跟隨美國隊長和鷹眼。萬達與她的哥哥很親近，直到她開始與幻視約會。

因為幻視並非人類，琵也達不認同他

inhuman and caused their first rift. Later on Pietro actually married his **rescuer**, Crystal who is also an inhuman. Pietro and Wanda eventually **mended** their **rift**.

們的關係。這件事造成他們兄妹之間的第一個裂痕。後來，琶也達娶了他的救命恩人水晶，水晶居然也是非人類。琶也達與萬達最終修補他們之間的裂痕。

卡漫精選字彙表

單字	詞性	中譯	單字	詞性	中譯
fellow	n.	人	rescuer	n.	救援者
brotherhood	n.	兄弟會	mend	v.	改善
extraterrestrial	adj.	外星球的	rift	n.	裂痕
alongside	adv.	沿著			

Up and Down Sides of the Superpower
超能力的優缺點

Quicksilver has an **impatient** personality. He once joined the U.S. government-**sponsored** X-Factor team. He told the psychologist how **frustrated** he was at dealing with a world where almost everyone and everything is slow and even stupid.

快銀有不耐煩的個性。他曾經參加了美國政府資助的X因素隊伍。他告訴心理學家，他在一個幾乎每個人，一切都是緩慢的，甚至愚蠢的的世界裡是多痛苦的一件事。

Quicksilver can not only run at a supersonic speed, he also has a fast **metabolism** so that he can recover from his wounds faster than an **ordinary** human being. Because of his speed, he can create **cyclone**-strength winds, run up walls and cross bodies of water. Quicksilver once lost his power of speed. Fortunately, Terrigen Mist, an inhuman, gave him some new

快銀不只能以超音速的速度運行，他也有一個快速的新陳代謝，使他的傷口可以比普通人更快地恢復。因為他的速度，他可以創造颶風強度的大風，跑上牆壁和跑過水面。快銀曾經一度失去了他的速度。幸運的是，泰

powers.

Quicksilver is able to **displace** himself out of **mainstream** time and space and go into the future. Although he performed his new power well, he still desired to get his former powers back, but he had no clue how to do so. It was not until one time he felt a desire to help a woman in **mortal** danger did he regain his power back. He saved the woman's life after all.

勒‧霧，一位非人類，給了他一些新的力量。

快銀能夠將自己擺脫主流的時間和空間到未來。雖然他很會執行他新的力量，但仍然希望能夠恢復他以前的力量，但他不知道如何做到這一點。直到有一次感到需要幫助一個生命遭遇危險的女人，他才重獲他的力量。他最終拯救了這位婦女的生命。

卡漫精選字彙表

單字	詞性	中譯	單字	詞性	中譯
impatient	adj.	沒耐心的	ordinary	adj.	普通的
sponsor	n.	發起者	cyclone	n.	氣旋
frustrate	v.	感到灰心	displace	v.	取代
supersonic	adj.	超音波的	mainstream	n.	主要傾向
metabolism	n.	新陳代謝	mortal	adj.	臨死的

必考字彙大回顧

卡漫超給力字彙表

單字	中譯	詞性	反義字	反義字中譯
discover	發現	*v.*	hide	隱藏
peculiar	罕見的	*adj.*	universal	普遍的
villager	村民	*n.*	foreigner	外國人
phenomenal	傑出的	*adj.*	unremarkable	不起眼的
uncontrollable	不可控制的	*adj.*	well-behaved	乖乖的
hex	施魔法	*v.*		
fellow	人	*n.*		
brotherhood	兄弟會	*n.*		
extraterrestrial	外星球的	*adj.*	terrestrial	地球上的
alongside	沿著	*adv.*	away	離開
rescuer	救援者	*n.*		
mend	改善	*v.*	destroy	破壞
rift	裂痕	*n.*	juncture	契機
impatient	沒耐心的	*adj.*	patient	有耐心的
sponsor	發起者	*n.*		
frustrate	感到灰心	*v.*	encourage	鼓勵
supersonic	超音波的	*adj.*		
metabolism	新陳代謝	*n.*		
ordinary	普通的	*adj.*	extraordinary	非凡的
cyclone	氣旋	*n.*		
displace	取代	*v.*	hold	保持

單字	中譯	詞性	反義字	反義字中譯
mainstream	主要傾向	*n.*	**unconventional**	非傳統的
mortal	臨死的	*adj.*	**immortal**	不朽

MP3 76

The Sadness of Being a Jew in the 1920s
20年代作為一個猶太人的悲哀

Born into a **Jewish** family in the late 1920s, Magneto and his family were faced with **discrimination** and **hardship** during the Nazi reign. His family escaped to Poland but were still captured by the Germans. They were later sent to the Warsaw Ghetto attempting to escape again but failed. Instead, his mother and sister were **executed**. Magneto on the other hand survived probably because the Germans saw his mutant powers. He was sent to Auschwitz, where he met his wife Magda.

The couple moved to the Ukrainian city of Vinnytsia. They

在20年代末期，出生於一個猶太家庭，萬磁王和他的家人在納粹掌權期間面臨歧視和苦難。他的家人逃到波蘭，但仍然被德國人所捕獲。他們後來被送到華沙猶太區，試圖再次逃跑，但沒有成功。他的母親和妹妹反而被處決。萬磁王卻倖存下來，因為德國人看到了他突變體的力量。他被送往奧斯威辛集中營，在那裡他遇到了他的妻子瑪格達。

這對夫婦搬到了烏克蘭的文尼斯。他

had a daughter named Anya. One day, a group of angry mob showed up which caused Magneto to **unleash** his power and accidentally burned down the house with Anya still inside. Magda was appalled by his irrational behavior and power and left him.

們有一個叫安雅的女兒。有一天，一群憤怒的暴徒出現了，造成萬磁王釋放他的力量並意外燒毀房子，而安雅還在裡面。瑪格達被他的不合乎常理的行為嚇到而離開他。

卡漫精選字彙表

單字	詞性	中譯	單字	詞性	中譯
Jewish	*n.*	猶太人	execute	*v.*	處死
discrimination	*n.*	歧視	unleash	*v.*	宣洩
hardship	*n.*	困苦			

01 劃時代的傳奇

02 不朽的英雄神話

03 無堅不摧背後的英雄血淚

04 永存於人們心中的英雄霸主

MP3 77

 Manipulate Magnetic Fields
操縱磁場

Since then, Magneto never tried to hide his power and his identity. He was proud to be a **mutant**. In fact, he is willing to use the deadly force to protect mutants. He believes that mutants will eventually be a dominant life form and will take over the world.

此後，萬磁王就沒有試圖掩蓋他的能力和他的身份。他很自豪身為一個突變體。事實上，他更願意利用致命的武力來保護突變體。他認為，突變體最終會取代人類，佔主導地位，接管世界。

Humankind will enter into **slavery**. He has no **intentions** to live peacefully with other kinds. To him, it's Mutant kind or nobody. With the power to control all forms of **magnetism**, Magneto is able to manipulate magnetic fields. He can also use his power in several different locations at once. He can also project any types of energy

人類將成為奴隸。他無意與其他生物和平共存。對他來說，這是突變體的天下。擁有能控制各種形式的磁的力量，萬磁王能夠操縱磁場。他可以同時在不同的地區使用他的力量，也可以投射一部份任

that are part of the **electromagnetic spectrum** such as radio waves, ultralights, and x-rays, and further more manipulate them.

He does have a weakness though. His body doesn't self-heal, and his power is **dependent** upon his physical condition. It means that after injury, his body is unable to **withstand** the **strain** of manipulating great amounts of magnetic forces. In fact, he becomes a normal human being.

何類型電磁頻譜的能量，如無線電波、超輕型和X射線，進一步操縱它們。

他確實有弱點。他的身體不會自癒，他的力量取決於他的身體狀況。這意味著，受傷後，他的身體是無法承受操縱大量磁力的應變。事實上，他將成為一般人。

卡漫精選字彙表

單字	詞性	中譯	單字	詞性	中譯
humankind	n.	人類	spectrum	n.	光譜
slavery	n.	奴隸	dependent	adj.	依靠的
intention	n.	意圖	withstand	v.	抵抗
magnetism	n.	磁力	strain	v.	拉緊
electromagnetic	adj.	電磁的			

Mutants Conquer the World
突變體征服世界

Magneto's first **villainous** act is attacking a U.S military base called Cape Citadel. He was driven off by the X-Men. He then gathered a group of **disillusioned** mutants who were full of anger and formed the Brotherhood of Evil. His kids, Quicksilver and Scarlet Witch were forced to be a part of the group as well. Although by then, neither of them knew they were biologically related. Magneto tried to **establish** a mutant homeland in the South but again was **foiled** by the X-Men. Magneto was then captured by the Stranger and was sent to another planet.

During that period of time, the

萬磁王的第一個惡棍行為是攻擊在海角城堡的一個美軍基地。他被 X 戰警趕走。然後，他聚集了一批失望且充滿憤怒的突變，並創造了邪惡兄弟會。他的孩子，快銀和猩紅巫婆也被迫成為集團的一部分。雖然在當時，他們不知道他們是有血緣關係的。萬磁王試圖在南方建立一個突變體的家園，但再次被X戰警挫敗。萬磁王之後被陌生人捕獲，並送往另一個星球。

那段時間，兄弟

Brotherhood fell apart. Quicksilver, Scarlet Witch and the other mutants **deserted** him. Magneto found his way to escape to Earth and **reassembled** the Brotherhood of Evil. His goal remains the same – Mutants will conquer the world!

會土崩瓦解。快銀、猩紅巫婆和其他突變體拋棄了他。萬磁王找到了自己掙脫的方式回到地球，並重組了邪惡兄弟會。他的目標仍然是相同的 - 突變體征服世界！

卡漫精選字彙表

單字	詞性	中譯	單字	詞性	中譯
villainous	*adj.*	惡棍的	foiled	*adj.*	有葉型式的
disillusion	*n.*	醒悟	desert	*v.*	拋棄
establish	*v.*	建立	reassemble	*v.*	再集合

01 劃時代的傳奇

02 不朽的英雄神話

03 無堅不摧背後的英雄血淚

04 永存於人們心中的英雄霸主

必考字彙大回顧

卡漫超給力字彙表

單字	中譯	詞性	反義字	反義字中譯
Jewish	猶太人	*n.*		
discrimination	歧視	*n.*	equity	公平
hardship	困苦	*n.*	comfort	安逸
execute	處死	*v.*		
unleash	宣洩	*v.*	hold	保持
humankind	人類	*n.*		
slavery	奴隸	*n.*	freedom	自由
intention	意圖	*n.*		
magnetism	磁力	*n.*		
electromagnetic	電磁的	*adj.*		
spectrum	光譜	*n.*		
dependent	依靠的	*adj.*	independent	獨立的
withstand	抵抗	*v.*	surrender	投降
strain	拉緊	*v.*	release	解放
villainous	惡棍的	*adj.*	good	好的
disillusion	醒悟	*n.*		
establish	建立	*v.*	destroy	破壞
foiled	有葉型式的	*adj.*		
desert	拋棄	*v.*	support	支持
reassemble	再集合	*v.*	go separate way	分道揚鑣

MP3 79

 From Japan to the United States
從日本到美國

The story of the Teenage Mutant Ninja Turtles, shortened as TMNT, starts with a rat in Japan. Hamato Yoshi, who was great at Ninjitsu owned a pet rat named Splinter. Splinter liked to **mimic** Yoshi when he practiced his Ninjitsu. One day, Yoshi accidentally killed his **rival** named Oroku Nagi during a fight. He then took Splinter and **immigrated** to the U.S.A. Nagi's brother eventually tracked him down and killed him, leaving Splinter on the street. Until one day, he saw a road accident **involving** a truck carrying **toxic** waste. Four turtles fell out of the truck into a **manhole**. Splinter followed them down and saw the four turtles covered in the **ooze**. He tried to help them and ended up

關於忍者龜的故事，縮寫為TMNT，始於日本的一隻老鼠。Hamato Yoshi 擅長忍術，他擁有一隻寵物鼠名為普林斯特。斯普林特最喜歡在他的主人練習忍術時模仿他。有一次，Yoshi在一次對戰中不慎殺死了他的對手 Oroku Nagi。隨後，他便與斯普林特移民到美國，Nagi 的弟弟最終找到了他，並將他殺死。使得斯普林特流落街頭。直到有一天，他看到一台運載有毒廢料卡車發生交通事故。四隻烏龜跌出了

with ooze all over himself too. The next day, not knowing exactly why, the five of them all had doubled in size and **intellect**. They all began walking **upright** and started to speak as human beings. Splinter named the 4 turtles after four Renaissance Italian artists. Knowing the outside world would not understand them, the five of them made their home **sewers** of New York City.

卡車進入了下水道。斯普林特跟著他們，只見四隻烏龜被蓋在軟泥之中。他試圖幫助他們，也讓自己滿布軟泥。第二天，不知道為什麼，他們五個的大小和智力都多了一倍。他們都開始直立行走，並開始說人話。斯普林特替四個烏龜依照文藝復興時期的意大利藝術家命名。他們了解外面的世界不會明白他們，因此他們五個生活在紐約市的下水道。

卡漫精選字彙表

單字	詞性	中譯	單字	詞性	中譯
mimic	v.	模仿	ooze	n.	滲出物
rival	n.	對手	intellect	n.	智力
immigrate	v.	移民（入）	upright	adj.	筆直的
involve	v.	捲入	renaissance	n.	文藝復興
toxic	adj.	有毒的	sewer	n.	下水道
manhole	n.	下水道			

Four Turtles, Four Personalities

四隻烏龜，四種性格

The four brothers look **similar** yet are very different. Donatello is the scientist, inventor, engineer, and **technological** genius. He wears a purple mask and fights with a Bo. He prefers to use his knowledge to solve **conflicts** instead of fighting.

Leonardo, on the other hand is the **tactical, courageous** leader. He wears a blue mask and fights with Katana. He often **bears** the **burden** of responsibility for his brothers, which commonly leads to conflict with Raphael. Michelangelo is the most **stereotypical** teenager of the team. He is free spirited and **goofy**. He is also the one that loves pizza the most. Michelangelo wears an

四個兄弟看似雷同，但卻有很大的不同。多納泰羅是科學家、發明家、工程師和技術天才。他戴著紫色面具並用棒子攻擊。他喜歡用自己的知識來解決衝突，而不是戰鬥。

李奧納多則是戰略性、勇敢的領導人。他戴著一件藍色的面具，用武士刀攻擊。他經常為他的兄弟承擔一切，這通常是導致他與拉斐爾發生衝突的原因。米開朗基羅是典型的青少年。他崇尚精神自由和滑稽。他也是最愛

orange mask and fights with a pair of Nunchucks. He also has a Southern Californian **accent**.

吃比薩餅的一位。米開朗基羅戴橘色面具並用雙截棍攻擊。他也有一個南加州的口音。

Raphael wears a red mask and fights with a pair of Sai. He is physically stronger than other three and much more **aggressive** as well. He sometimes fights with his brothers, but he is also **intensely** loyal to his brothers and sensei.

拉斐爾則是戴著紅色面具和用一對刀劍攻擊。他身體比其他三個都強壯，也更加積極好鬥。他有時與他的兄弟打架，但他也強烈地忠於自己的兄弟和老師。

卡漫精選字彙表

單字	詞性	中譯	單字	詞性	中譯
similar	*n.*	雷同	burden	*n.*	重擔
technological	*adj.*	技術的	stereotypical	*adj.*	陳規的
conflict	*v.*	衝突	goofy	*adj.*	滑稽的
tactical	*adj.*	戰術的	accent	*n.*	口音
courageous	*adj.*	英勇的	aggressive	*adj.*	好鬥的
bear	*v.*	支持	intensely	*adv.*	強烈地

MP3 81

Reveal the Origin and Ask for Avenge
說出身世的由來並要求復仇

When the turtles were 13 years old, Splinter thought their training was complete and they were ready to face off against the street gang, Purple Dragon.

當烏龜們13歲時，斯普林特認為他們的培訓已經完成，並已準備好面對反派的街頭幫派，紫金神龍。

He told them of their **origin** and told them that he was already too old to battle. He asked the turtles to **avenge** the death of his old master.

他告訴他們，他們的原生並表示他已經太老無法戰鬥。他要求烏龜們替他的老主人報復。

The TMNT successfully took down Saki and the Purple Dragon.

忍者龜成功的拿下Saki和紫金神龍。

They then started to use their skills to battle criminals and evil overlords while attempting to remain hidden from society.

然後，他們就開始用他們的能力戰鬥罪犯和邪惡的統治者，並試圖躲藏在社會之中。

Interestingly, their favorite food is pizza.

有趣的是，他們最喜歡的食物是披薩。

卡漫精選字彙表

單字	詞性	中譯	單字	詞性	中譯
origin	*n.*	出身	avenge	*v.*	替……報仇

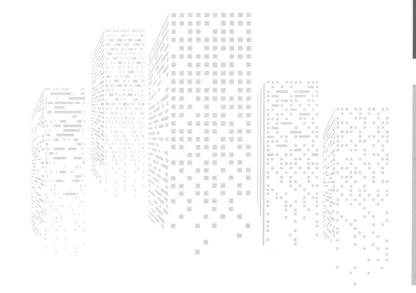

必考字彙大回顧

卡漫超給力字彙表

單字	中譯	詞性	反義字	反義字中譯
mimic	模仿	*v.*	be original	原創
rival	對手	*n.*	ally	盟友
immigrate	移民（入）	*v.*	emigrate	移民（出）
involve	捲入	*v.*	dissociate	使……分開
toxic	有毒的	*adj.*	harmless	無害的
manhole	下水道	*n.*		
ooze	滲出物	*n.*		
intellect	智力	*n.*		
upright	筆直的	*adj.*	level	水平的
renaissance	文藝復興	*n.*		
sewer	下水道	*n.*		
similar	雷同	*n.*	different	不同
technological	技術的	*adj.*		
conflict	衝突	*v.*	concur	同意
tactical	戰術的	*adj.*		
courageous	英勇的	*adj.*	cowardly	膽小的
bear	支持	*v.*	disregard	漠視
burden	重擔	*n.*		
stereotypical	陳規的	*adj.*		
goofy	滑稽的	*adj.*	sensible	明智的
accent	口音	*n.*		

單字	中譯	詞性	反義字	反義字中譯
aggressive	好鬥的	*adj.*	**peaceful**	平靜的
intensely	強烈地	*adv.*	**mildly**	輕度地
origin	出身	*n.*		
avenge	替……報仇	*v.*	**forgive**	原諒

part4

永存於人們心中的英雄霸主

學習進度表

Unit 28 Shredder
許瑞德
- ☐ 28-1 成長背景
- ☐ 28-2 四人聯手
- ☐ 28-3 展開決鬥
- ☐ 必考字彙大回顧

Unit 29 Wolverine 金鋼狼
- ☐ 29-1 成長背景
- ☐ 29-2 終止羅慕盧斯的惡行
- ☐ 29-3 癒合因子
- ☐ 必考字彙大回顧

Unit 30 Sabretooth 劍齒虎
- ☐ 30-1 成長背景
- ☐ 30-2 金鋼狼頭號敵人
- ☐ 30-3 成長背景
- ☐ 必考字彙大回顧

Unit 31 Hawkeye 鷹眼
- ☐ 31-1 成長背景
- ☐ 31-2 後悔自己的決定
- ☐ 31-3 巔峰能力
- ☐ 必考字彙大回顧

Unit 32 Trick Shot 捷射
- ☐ 32-1 成長背景
- ☐ 32-2 射殺兄長
- ☐ 32-3 新身分「鷹眼」
- ☐ 必考字彙大回顧

Unit 33 Black Widow
黑寡婦
- ☐ 33-1 成長背景
- ☐ 33-2 真正的寡婦
- ☐ 33-3 獨立的超級英雄
- ☐ 必考字彙大回顧

Unit 34 The Red Guardian
紅衛士
- ☐ 34-1 成長背景
- ☐ 34-2 技術高超的運動員
- ☐ 34-3 遇見黑寡婦
　　　　和美國上尉
- ☐ 必考字彙大回顧

Unit 35 The Hulk 浩克
- ☐ 35-1 成長背景
- ☐ 35-2 無限的力量
- ☐ 35-3 總統的特赦
- ☐ 必考字彙大回顧

Unit 36 The Leader 首腦
- ☐ 36-1 成長背景
- ☐ 36-2 統治世界的夢想
- ☐ 36-3 重拾力量
- ☐ 必考字彙大回顧

是否能晉升為超能字彙英雄？

★完成10小節 → 「肉雞小英雄」

★完成27小節 → 「小小英雄達人」

★完成36小節 → 「傳奇英雄」

Unit 28
Shredder 許瑞德

28-1　成長背景

MP3 82 ▶

 ### *The Most Skilled Warrior*
最熟練的戰士

Oroku Saki is a normal human with great strength, **stamina**, and agility. He is a great martial arts fighter and brilliant with **aptitudes** in a wide variety of sciences. When he was a little boy, his respectful older brother Oroku Nagi was killed by Hamato Toshi in a battle for a woman Tang Shen. Saki swore the revenge and **enrolled** in the Foot Clan.

He soon rose up the ranks and became their most **skilled** warrior. He was also chosen to lead the American **branch** of the Foot in New York at the age of 18.

Oroku Saki是一個普通人類，但具有巨大的力量，耐力和敏捷性。他是一個很好的武術高手，也在各種科學性向上都很聰明。當他還是一個小男孩時，他敬愛的哥哥Oroku Yoshi在一場為一個名為唐軒的女人的戰鬥中被Hamato Yoshiko殺死。Saki發誓報復，並報名參加了腳族。

他很快的在排名中名列前茅，並成為他們最熟練的戰士。他也被選為領導在紐約腳族的美國分支

Although he was still very young, he **adopted** the identity of the Shredder and murdered both Yoshi and Shen.

His cold heart made him very successful in the criminal circle of New York. He basically built the **formidable** criminal **empire** which was involved in drug smuggling, arms running, and assassinations. One day, when he was doing some shady business, a sai **blade** came through the window with a note on it. The note said that someone wanted to challenge Shredder to a **duel** to the death.

時，只有18歲。雖然他還很年輕，他採用了許瑞德這個身份，並謀殺了Yoshi與唐軒。

他的冷血，使他在紐約的犯罪圈裡非常的成功。他基本上建立了強大的犯罪帝國，並參與毒品走私、軍火運行和暗殺。有一天，當他在做一些見不得人的事業時，一個帶有字條的刀從窗口飛進來。這個字條説明了有人想挑戰許瑞德，決鬥到死。

01 劃時代的傳奇

02 不朽的英雄神話

03 無堅不摧背後的英雄血淚

04 永存於人們心中的英雄霸主

卡漫精選字彙表

單字	詞性	中譯	單字	詞性	中譯
stamina	*n.*	精力	adopt	*v.*	採取
aptitude	*n.*	傾向	formidable	*adj.*	令人畏懼的
enroll	*v.*	報名	empire	*n.*	帝國
skill	*n.*	能力	blade	*n.*	刀刃
branch	*n.*	分行	duel	*n.*	對抗

Finish It
結束他

Shredder of course showed up at the battle, but surprisingly, he saw 4 giant turtles waiting for him. The turtles took down the Foot Ninjas and Shredder decided to take on the turtles by himself.

Shredder was indeed very good at martial arts. The four needed to battle him together in order to get a chance to succeed. At the end, Leonardo scored a lucky shot by **plunging** his sword through the Shredder's **torso**. As a ninja, Shredder would not want to live with shame. He asked them to "finish it", but Leonardo told him to take down his own life. Shredder responded that if he must take his own life, he will take the turtles

許瑞德當然出現在戰鬥的地點,但令人驚訝的,他看到的是四隻巨型烏龜在等著他。烏龜們拿下了腳族忍者。許瑞德決定自己對付烏龜。

許瑞德確實非常好武。四隻烏龜需要一起對戰他,才會有成功的機會。最後,李奧納多幸運地一劍插進許瑞德的軀幹裡。作為一個忍者,許瑞德不想忍辱偷生。他要他們「結束它」,但李奧納多要他自己結束自己的生命。許瑞德回應,如果他必須結束自己的

lives with him.

He took out a Thermite Bomb which would **wipe** the rooftop clean of all life. Donatello quickly used his Bo to knock Shredder and the bomb off the roof. As he fell the bomb exploded and tore Shredder to pieces.

生命，他也會一起結束烏龜們的生命。

他拿出一個可以結束屋頂下所有生命的鋁熱劑炸彈。多納泰羅迅速地用自己的棍棒將許瑞德和炸彈打往半空中。當他落下時，炸彈爆炸，將許瑞德炸成碎片。

卡漫精選字彙表

單字	詞性	中譯	單字	詞性	中譯
plunge	*v.*	插入	wipe	*v.*	擦乾
torso	*n.*	軀幹			

01 劃時代的傳奇

02 不朽的英雄神話

03 無堅不摧背後的英雄血淚

04 永存於人們心中的英雄霸主

Came Back to Life
復活

　　Almost a year after on Christmas eve, Leonardo went out for a training and was attacked by a **literal** army of Foot Soldiers. Leonardo was badly injured and crashed through the window while going home.

　　He told the rest of the team, the Shredder is back. The Foot Clan soon came **bursting** into the house and an **intense** battle started. **Unexpectedly**, Raphael's friend Casey Jones showed up and battled Shredder directly.

　　The building caught on fire, and before the police and the fire trucks **approached**, Shredder ordered his people to **retreat**, but

　　將近一年後的聖誕節，李奧納多出外訓練時被腳族的軍隊攻擊。李奧納多受到重傷，並溜過窗口趕回家。

　　他告訴其他人，許瑞德又回來了。腳族很快就衝進了屋子，激烈的戰鬥開始了。沒想到，拉斐爾的朋友凱西・瓊斯出現了，直接與許瑞德開始交戰。

　　建築物開始著火，警察和消防車到之前，許瑞德命令他的人撤退。但是他承

he promised he would come back.　　諾，他會再回來。

卡漫精選字彙表

單字	詞性	中譯	單字	詞性	中譯
literal	*adj.*	不誇張的	unexpectedly	*adv.*	意外地
burst	*v.*	爆炸	approach	*v.*	接近
intense	*adj.*	劇烈的	retreat	*n.*	撤退

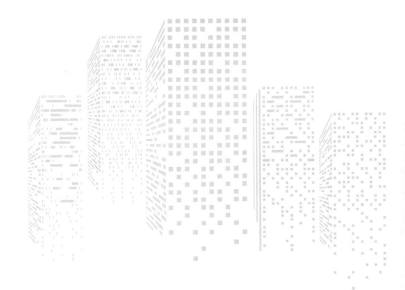

卡漫超給力字彙表

單字	中譯	詞性	反義字	反義字中譯
stamina	精力	*n.*	frailty	脆弱
aptitude	傾向	*n.*		
enroll	報名	*v.*	expel	驅逐
skill	能力	*n.*		
branch	分行	*n.*		
adopt	採取	*v.*	reject	拒絕
formidable	令人畏懼的	*adj.*	unthreatening	無威脅的
empire	帝國	*n.*		
blade	刀刃	*n.*		
duel	對抗	*n.*		
plunge	插入	*v.*	pull out	拔出
torso	軀幹	*n.*		
wipe	擦乾	*v.*	dirty	弄髒
literal	不誇張的	*adj.*	figurative	象徵的
burst	爆炸	*v.*		
intense	劇烈的	*adj.*	moderate	適度的
unexpectedly	意外地	*adv.*	predictably	不出所料的
approach	接近	*v.*	evade	逃避
retreat	撤退	*n.*	continue	繼續

MP3 85

The Discovery of the Claws
狼爪的發現

The son of rich farm owners John and Elizabeth Howlett, James Howlett was born in Cold Lake, Alberta, Canada. One day, James happened to see an incident that the groundkeeper, Thomas Logan killed John Howlett. It was the first time James' claws **extended** from the backs of his hands and he attacked the **intruders** with **uncharacteristic ferocity**. He killed Thomas Logan, and scarring Dog's face with three claw marks. James later on adopted the name "Logan" to hide his identity. Logan and his childhood playmate, Rose eventually fell in love.

富有農場主人約翰和伊麗莎白·豪利特的兒子,詹姆斯·豪利特出生在加拿大阿爾伯塔省的冷湖。詹姆斯碰巧看到場地管理人,湯瑪斯·洛根殺害約翰·豪利。這是第一次,詹姆斯的爪子從他的手背延伸,他異常兇猛的攻擊入侵者。他殺死了湯瑪斯·洛根,並在道格的臉上留下三個爪痕。詹姆斯後來就採用了「洛根」這個名字,以隱藏自己的身份。洛根和他的童年玩伴羅絲最終墜入愛河。

However, during an incident while Dog, the son of Thomas Logan was battling with Logan, he accidentally killed Rose with his claws. He had no choice but to leave the **colony** and live in the wilderness **among** real wolves. Logan is a mutant. He has his signature wolf claws and possesses animal-keen sense, enhanced physical capabilities, and powerful **regenerative** ability known as a healing factor.

然而，在湯瑪斯·洛根的兒子道格與洛根對戰時，意外發生了，他的爪子偶然地殺害了羅絲。他只好離開群體，生活在真正荒野的狼群中。洛根是一個突變體。他有著他著名的狼爪，擁有動物敏銳的感覺，進階的體能，和稱為癒合因子強大的再生能力。

卡漫精選字彙表

單字	詞性	中譯	單字	詞性	中譯
playmate	*n.*	玩伴	uncharacteristic	*adj.*	不尋常的
groundskeeper	*n.*	土地管理者	ferocity	*n.*	殘暴
abusive	*adj.*	辱罵的	colony	*n.*	群體
extend	*v.*	延伸	among	*prep.*	在……中間
intruder	*n.*	侵入者	regenerative	*adj.*	新生的

Wolverine 金鋼狼

29-2 終止羅慕盧斯的惡行

MP3 86

Joining the Superhero Teams
加入超級英雄團隊

While he was a member of Team X, he was given a **false** memory **implants**. It was not until he joined the Canadian Defense Ministry did he break free of the mental control. He then started to work as an intelligence **operative** for the Canadian government and became the first Canadian superhero, Wolverine. Wolverine was later on recruited by Professor Charles Xavier to the superhero-mutant team, the X-Men.

One time, it was not until that the supervillain Magneto removed the adamantium from Wolverine's **skeleton** did he first realize that his claws are actually bone. It took him a long time to heal from the **massive trauma** which caused his

爾後，他在軍隊裡被植入了假的記憶體。直到他加入加拿大國防部才掙脫了精神控制。然後，他開始作為一個情報人員並和加拿大政府合作，成為加拿大的第一位超級英雄，金剛狼。金剛狼後來被查爾斯·澤維爾教授招募到超級英雄突變隊，X戰警。

有一次，在萬磁王去除了金剛狼骨骼裡的亞德曼金屬，金剛狼才第一次意識到，他的爪子實際上是骨頭。因為大面積的創傷，他花了很長

healing factor to burn out. Wolverine returned back to the X-Men. Once, the villain Apocalypse caught Wolverine, and brainwashed him into becoming the Horseman Death. Wolverine **overcame** the programming and returned back to the X-Men. He then joined the Avengers. Wolverine finally discovered he had a son named Daken. By then, Daken was brainwashed and was working for the villain Romulus. Wolverine made it his mission to rescue his son and stop Romulus from harming anyone else anymore.

的時間癒合傷口。金剛狼回到X戰警隊。另一次，千年老妖抓到了金剛狼，企圖將他洗腦，說服他成為死亡騎士。金剛狼克服了編程，並返回X戰警隊。之後，他加入了復仇者。金剛狼終於發現他有一個叫達肯的兒子。屆時，達肯已被洗腦，並努力為惡棍羅穆盧斯工作。金剛狼設立了他的使命，他要拯救他的兒子和阻止羅慕盧斯傷害其他任何人。

01 劃時代的傳奇

02 不朽的英雄神話

03 無堅不摧背後的英雄血淚

04 永存於人們心中的英雄霸主

卡漫精選字彙表

單字	詞性	中譯	單字	詞性	中譯
aware	*adj.*	知道的	skeleton	*n.*	骨骼
parachute	*n.*	降落傘	massive	*adj.*	大規模的
battalion	*n.*	軍隊	trauma	*n.*	外傷
false	*adj.*	不真實的	overcome	*v.*	克服
operative	*adj.*	操作的			

Unit 29
Wolverine 金鋼狼

29-3　癒合因子

 The Death of Wolverine
金剛狼之死

In 2014, there was a **virus** from the microverse which can turn down Wolverine's healing factor and his enemies will be able to kill him.

Other Superhero's such as Mister Fantastic offered to work on finding a means of **reactivating** his healing factor.

However, before the solution was found, Wolverine was killed by the hardening Adamantium. The X-Men and the team were heartbroken over what happened to Wolverine.

2014年，微細病毒可以取消金剛狼的癒合因子，他的敵人就可以殺死他。

其他超級英雄的，如奇幻人開始尋找讓癒合因子復活的方式。

但是在發現該溶液之前，金剛狼已經被硬化的亞德曼金屬所殺死。X戰警和團隊對於金剛狼所發生的事傷透了心。

卡漫精選字彙表

單字	詞性	中譯	單字	詞性	中譯
virus	*n.*	病毒	reactivate	*v.*	重新啟動

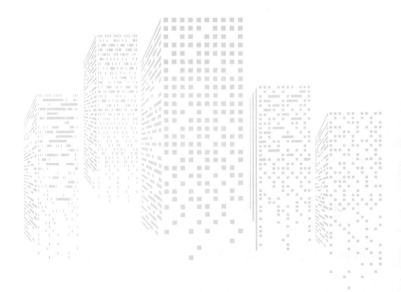

01 劃時代的傳奇

02 不朽的英雄神話

03 無堅不摧背後的英雄血淚

04 永存於人們心中的英雄霸主

卡漫超給力字彙表

單字	中譯	詞性	反義字	反義字中譯
playmate	玩伴	*n.*	enemy	敵人
groundskeeper	土地管理者	*n.*		
abusive	辱罵的	*adj.*	polite	有禮貌的
extend	延伸	*v.*	curtail	縮短
intruder	侵入者	*n.*		
uncharacteristic	不尋常的	*adj.*	typical	典型的
ferocity	殘暴	*n.*	gentleness	溫柔
colony	群體	*n.*		
among	在……中間	*prep.*	away from	遠離
regenerative	新生的	*adj.*	degenerative	退化的
aware	知道的	*adj.*	unaware	不知道
parachute	降落傘	*n.*		
battalion	軍隊	*n.*		
false	不真實的	*adj.*	real	真實的
operative	操作的	*adj.*	inactive	
skeleton	骨骼	*n.*		
massive	大規模的	*adj.*	insignificant	微不足道的
trauma	外傷	*n.*		
overcome	克服	*v.*		
virus	病毒	*n.*		
reactivate	重新啟動	*v.*	deactivate	關閉

MP3 88

 When the Mutation was Manifested
當突變顯現時

When Sabretooth was a little boy, he **accidentally** killed his brother over a piece of pie. That was the first time the mutation was manifested. His **canine** teeth grew much larger and sharper **akin** to a big cat, and his finger and toenails turned into 20 **retractable talons**.

當劍齒虎還是一個小男孩時，他偶然地為了一塊派殺害了他的弟弟。這是第一次他突變的因子顯現出來。他的犬齒變得更大更清晰，類似於一隻大型貓科，他的手指和腳趾甲變成了20根可以伸縮的爪子。

He also got claws which were so sharp that could cut through most types of **flesh** and **structure**. His father was terrified and locked him in a **cellar**. He also built an automatic system that would pull out Victor's "devil teeth" in an attempt to **purge** his "demons." Victor was treated as an animal for

他還擁有了犀利到可以切過大多數類型的肉和結構的爪子。他的父親嚇壞了，把他鎖在地窖裡。他還建立了一個自動系統來自動拔除維克特的「魔鬼牙齒」，企圖清除他的

years until one day, he broke the cellar and killed his father.

After leaving his own house, he worked for the railroad at the age of fifteen. One day during his work, he was picked on by a **belligerent** older man. Sabretooth couldn't control himself and **gutted** him from crotching his throat with his claws.

「心魔。」維克特多年來被視為動物，直到有一天，他衝破了地窖，殺死他的父親。

離開自己的房子後，15歲的他便在鐵路工作。在他工作期間的有一天，他被一個好戰的老男人欺負。劍齒虎無法控制自己，他用他的爪子，將對方從胯下割破到他的喉結。

卡漫精選字彙表

單字	詞性	中譯	單字	詞性	中譯
mutation	n.	突變	flesh	n.	肉
manifest	v.	表現	structure	n.	結構體
accidentally	adv.	偶然地	cellar	n.	地窖
canine	adj.	犬的	purge	v.	使淨化
akin	adj.	類似的	belligerent	adj.	好鬥的
retractable	adj.	可伸縮的	gut	v.	損毀
talon	n.	爪子			

MP3 89 ▶

 Way Back in 1912
回朔到1912年

As Wolverine's number 1 enemy, Sabretooth and Wolverine's battles go all the way back to 1912. Sabretooth started to work for a man by the name of Hudson. Hudson ordered him to attack a Blackfoot **tribe** where Wolverine was living in.

Sabretooth ended up murdering Wolverine's lover, Silverfox. Years later, Sabretooth became **involved** with a group which killed Wolverine's wife Itsu and the **abduction** of her son. Sabretooth then was recruited into the Avengers in 1959.

A few years later, Sabretooth

作為金剛狼的第一號敵人，劍齒虎和金剛狼的戰鬥可以一路回溯到1912年，當劍齒虎開始為一個名為哈德森的人工作時。哈德森命令他攻擊黑腳部落，當時金剛狼正好生活在其中。

劍齒虎最終謀殺金剛狼的愛人，銀狐。多年以後，劍齒虎參與殺害了金剛狼的妻子Itsu和她兒子綁架案的一群。劍齒虎在1959年被招入復仇者。

幾年後，因為一

became a member of Team X with Wolverine and Maverick for a Russian mission, although it didn't last long. He later on joined the Marauders to **massacre** the Morlocks. Once again, Sabretooth battled with Wolverine.

個俄羅斯的任務,劍齒虎和金剛狼、獨行俠一起成為X小組的一員,雖然並沒有持續多久。後來,他就加入了掠奪者以屠殺莫洛克人。劍齒虎再度的與金剛狼作戰。

卡漫精選字彙表

單字	詞性	中譯	單字	詞性	中譯
tribe	*n.*	部落	abduction	*n.*	綁架
involve	*v.*	涉及	massacre	*n.*	大屠殺

Time to Put an End
是時候做個了結

Hating the fact that he couldn't control his **murderous rages**, Sabretooth once found a telepath named Birdy who can help him calm down and control his emotion. The situation was good for some time, until one day his son killed Birdy. Sabretooth lost all his control. Professor X tried to help him and kept him in the **Mansion**. However, he wasn't there for long. Sabretooth fought his way out and **rejoined** the Hound Program to kill! Time after time, Sabretooth saw Wolverine as his number 1 target. He traveled around the world to gain more power and strength in order to take Wolverine down. Wolverine thought it was time to put an end to Sabretooth so he asked Cyclops

厭惡無法控制自己殺氣肆虐的事實，劍齒虎有一次發現了一位會心靈感應的人，名為博蒂，可以幫助他冷靜下來，控制住自己的情緒。情況好轉了一段時間，直到有一天他的兒子殺死了博蒂。劍齒虎失去了所有的控制。教授試圖幫助他，並將他留在官邸。不過，他在那裡待不久。劍齒虎找到他逃出去的方法，並重新加入獵犬計劃來殺人！一次又一次，劍齒虎視金剛狼為他的頭號目標。他周遊世界各地以獲得更多的

for the Muramasa Blade which can **nullify** healing factors.

Wolverine chased down the **rabid** Sabretooth and sliced off his arm. Even though Sabretooth was badly injured, he wouldn't **surrender**. Wolverine ended up killing him. Later on, Professor X **revealed** to Wolverine that Sabretooth was actually his first choice to be a member of the X-men.

權力和力量，讓他可以將金剛狼拿下。金剛狼認為這是結束劍齒虎的時候，於是詢問獨眼巨人，向他借了可以剔除癒合能力的「村正妖刀」。

金剛狼追到狂熱的劍齒虎並割下他的手臂。儘管劍齒虎受了重傷，他也不投降。金剛狼最終殺害了他。後來，Ｘ教授透露給金剛狼知道，實際上他認為能成為Ｘ戰警成員的第一選擇其實是劍齒虎。

卡漫精選字彙表

單字	詞性	中譯	單字	詞性	中譯
murderous	*adj.*	蓄意謀殺的	nullify	*v.*	廢止
rage	*n.*	憤怒	rabid	*adj.*	瘋狂的
mansion	*n.*	官邸	surrender	*v.*	投降
rejoin	*v.*	歸隊	reveal	*v.*	揭示

卡漫超給力字彙表

單字	中譯	詞性	反義字	反義字中譯
mutation	突變	*n.*	sameness	千篇一律
manifest	表現	*v.*	hide	隱藏
accidentally	偶然地	*adv.*	on purpose	故意的
canine	犬的	*adj.*		
akin	類似的	*adj.*	unlike	不同的
retractable	可伸縮的	*adj.*		
talon	爪子	*n.*		
flesh	肉	*n.*		
structure	結構體	*n.*		
cellar	地窖	*n.*		
purge	使淨化	*v.*	dirty	弄髒
belligerent	好鬥的	*adj.*	easygoing	隨和的
gut	損毀	*v.*	protect	保護
tribe	部落	*n.*		
involve	涉及	*v.*	dissociate	游離
abduction	綁架	*n.*		
massacre	大屠殺	*n.*		
murderous	蓄意謀殺的	*adj.*		
rage	憤怒	*n.*	happiness	幸福
mansion	官邸	*n.*		
rejoin	歸隊	*v.*		

單字	中譯	詞性	反義字	反義字中譯
nullify	廢止	*v.*	**keep**	保持
rabid	瘋狂的	*adj.*	**apathetic**	冷淡的
surrender	投降	*v.*	**fight**	戰鬥
reveal	揭示	*v.*	**conceal**	隱藏

01 劃時代的傳奇

02 不朽的英雄神話

03 無堅不摧背後的英雄血淚

04 永存於人們心中的英雄霸主

MP3 91

Inspired by Iron Man
鋼鐵人的啟發

Born in Waverly, Iowa, Clint Barton had a brother named Barney Barton. The borthers eventually joined the Carson Carnival of Traveling Wonders.

出生於愛荷華州為弗利，柯林·巴頓有一個名為巴尼·巴頓的哥哥。兄弟倆最終加入旅遊奇蹟的卡森移動樂園。

One day, Clint accidentally found out that the Swordsman was **embezzling** money from the carnival. Clint was terrified and tried to report to the owner. However, before he could do so, he was already beaten up by the Swordsman before he escaped. Even so, Barney didn't have any **sympathy** on Clint. Instead, Barney blamed Clint for not sharing the **fortune** and **abandoned** him since.

有一天，柯林無意間發現劍客笑挪用樂園的資金。柯林嚇壞了，並試圖向業主報告。但是，他還沒來得及這樣做前，就已經被劍客毆打，劍客也逃跑了。即便如此，巴尼並沒有同情柯林。相反的，巴尼指責柯林沒有共享財富，因此拋棄了他。

Clint left the Carson Carnival

柯林離開了卡森

and started to use his natural archery skills to work in various carnivals as "Hawkeye". He was also known as "The World's Greatest Marksman." Once during his **performance**, he **witnessed** Iron Man saving lives. He was so **inspired** and soon decided to become a costumed crime fighter.

移動樂園，並開始利用他與生俱來的射箭技能，以「鷹眼」的名號在不同的嘉年華工作。在他表演的期間，也被稱為是「世界上最偉大的射手」。有一次，他親眼目睹了鋼鐵人拯救生命。他因此精神振奮，很快就決定成為一個喬裝的打擊犯罪戰士。

卡漫精選字彙表

單字	詞性	中譯	單字	詞性	中譯
carnival	*n.*	流動遊藝團	abandon	*v.*	離棄
embezzle	*v.*	挪用	performance	*n.*	演出
sympathy	*n.*	同情	witness	*v.*	見證
fortune	*n.*	財富	inspire	*v.*	啟發

MP3 92

 From Enemies to Partners
從敵人到成為合作夥伴

However, at the first night on **patrol,** he was mistaken for a criminal by police and was hunted down. He met the Black Widow, a spy for the Soviet Union. She falsely led him to believe he could get the technology from Iron man if he defeats him.

然而，在巡邏的第一個晚上，他被警方誤認為罪犯而被追殺。在逃跑時，他遇到了蘇聯間諜黑寡婦。他很快地愛上了她。黑寡婦使他相信他希望可以打敗鋼鐵人，並從他那裡偷技術。

Later on, he **wised up** who the Black Widow really is and how she was trying to manipulate his thoughts. Hawkeye **regretted** his decision and hoped to join the Avengers. He broke in to the Avengers Mansion and displayed his powers with the help from the **butler,** Edwin Jarvis. Iron Man saw how serious Hawkeye was about

後來，他識破了黑寡婦的真為人，也了解到她是如何試圖操縱他的想法。鷹眼後悔自己的決定，並希望加入復仇者。他闖進了復仇者大廈，並在管家愛德恩·賈維斯的幫助下顯示他的能力。鋼鐵人看到

becoming a hero. Therefore, he **vouched** for Hawkeye to be a member of the Avengers.

He was once **romantically** involved with the Scarlet Witch and was met with **hostility** from her brother, Quicksilver. The relationship didn't last because Hawkeye was still in love with the Black Widow. Hawkeye once **doubted** Captain America's leadership before, but over time he came to respect him and see him as a mentor.

鷹眼是多麼認真希望成為一位英雄。因此，他擔保了鷹眼成為復仇者的成員。

鷹眼也曾與猩紅巫婆有著浪漫的關係，因此而和她哥哥快銀之間有了敵意。這段感情並沒有持續，因為鷹眼還是愛著黑寡婦。鷹眼曾經懷疑過美國隊長的領導，但隨著時間的推移，他變得尊重他，並視他為導師。

卡漫精選字彙表

單字	詞性	中譯	單字	詞性	中譯
patrol	*n.*	巡邏	vouch	*v.*	擔保
flee	*v.*	逃跑	romantically	*adv.*	浪漫地
wise up	*v.*	了解	hostility	*n.*	敵意
regret	*v.*	後悔	doubt	*v.*	懷疑
butler	*n.*	男管家			

MP3 93

Superhero without Superhuman Powers
沒有超能力的超級英雄

Even though Hawkeye doesn't have superhuman powers, he is at the **peak** of human conditions.

雖然鷹眼沒有超能力，但是他人類能力條件卻是處於最高峰。

Being trained in the circus since he was a kid, he is also an **exceptional** fencer, acrobat and marksman.

因為在孩童時期便在馬戲團裡接受訓練，他因此也是一個出色的擊劍運動員、雜技演員和射手。

Hawkeye uses a 250 pounds-force draw weight bow which no one else is capable of drawing the string to **launch** an arrow.

鷹眼採用的是250磅中的畫弓，沒有人能夠拉得動他的弓箭來發射箭頭。

Hawkeye was also trained by Captain America in martial arts and hand-to-hand **combat** so he has no problem fighting the villains without his weapons. He even has

鷹眼也被美國隊長訓練武術和肉搏戰術，因此就算沒有武器，他可以與敵人對戰。他甚至有能夠把

a **reputation** for being able to turn any object into a weapon.

任何物體變為武器的聲譽。

卡漫精選字彙表

單字	詞性	中譯	單字	詞性	中譯
peak	*n.*	巔峰	combat	*n.*	戰鬥
exceptional	*adj.*	優秀的	reputation	*n.*	聲譽
launch	*v.*	發射			

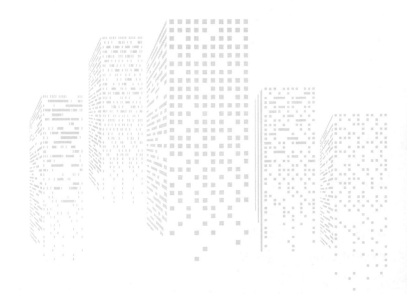

01 劃時代的傳奇

02 不朽的英雄神話

03 無堅不摧背後的英雄血淚

04 永存於人們心中的英雄霸主

必考字彙大回顧

卡漫超給力字彙表

單字	中譯	詞性	反義字	反義字中譯
orphanage	孤兒院	*n.*		
carnival	流動遊藝團	*n.*		
archer	射手	*n.*		
embezzle	挪用	*v.*	compensate	賠償
sympathy	同情	*n.*	cruelty	殘酷
fortune	財富	*n.*	debt	債務
abandon	離棄	*v.*	keep	保持
performance	演出	*n.*		
witness	見證	*v.*	hide	隱藏
inspire	啟發	*v.*	discourage	使沮喪
patrol	巡邏	*n.*		
flee	逃跑	*v.*	face	面對
wise up	了解	*v.*	ignorant	無知的
regret	後悔	*v.*	endorse	認同
butler	男管家	*n.*		
vouch	擔保	*v.*	reject	拒絕
romantically	浪漫地	*adv.*		
hostility	敵意	*n.*	friendliness	友好
doubt	懷疑	*v.*	certainty	肯定
peak	巔峰	*n.*	bottom	底部
exceptional	優秀的	*adj.*	ordinary	普通的

單字	中譯	詞性	反義字	反義字中譯
launch	發射	*v.*	**catch**	抓住
combat	戰鬥	*n.*	**give in**	讓步
reputation	聲譽	*n.*		

01 劃時代的傳奇

02 不朽的英雄神話

03 無堅不摧背後的英雄血淚

04 永存於人們心中的英雄霸主

MP3 94

Growing Up in the Shadow
在陰影中成長

Growing up with Hawkeye in the carnival, Barney has been living in the shadow. Without a mentor like the Swordsman, Barney was working as his brother's **assistant**.

He became jealous and **distant** from Clint. One time, when Clint found out that Swordsman was embezzling money from the carnival, Barney **condemned** Clint for going against Swordsman.

Barney got tired of the circus life and decided to join the US army. He did ask his brother to join him. Barney gave Clint an **ultimatum**, to join him or lose his brother. Barney waited for his

　在移動樂園中與鷹眼一起長大，巴尼一直生活在陰影之中。沒有一個像劍客一樣的良師益友，巴尼工作就是作為弟弟的助手。

　他嫉妒柯林並開始遠離柯林。有一次，當柯林發現劍士從移動樂園裡挪用資金，巴尼竟然譴責柯林特違背劍客。

　巴尼厭倦了馬戲團的生活，並決定加入美國軍隊。他要他的弟弟和他一起。巴尼給了柯林最後通牒，要他加入或失去

brother to show up, but Clint never did. Barney left **disappointedly**.

他的兄弟。巴尼等著弟弟露面，但柯林並沒有。巴尼失望地離開。

卡漫精選字彙表

單字	詞性	中譯	單字	詞性	中譯
assistant	*n.*	助理	ultimatum	*n.*	最後通牒
distance	*v.*	使遠離	disappointedly	*adv.*	失望地
condemn	*v.*	譴責			

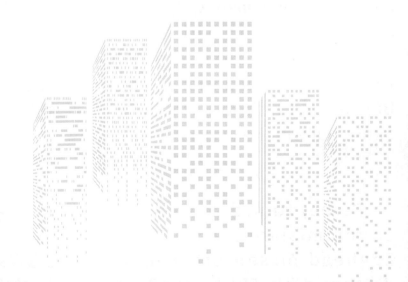

As an Undercover Agent
作為臥底

Barney later on became a FBI Agent after his **stint** in the Army. Most of the time, he worked **undercover**. Once, he was working undercover as a **bodyguard** for a criminal named Marko.

巴尼他在退出軍隊後，後來成為FBI探員。大多數時候，他身為臥底。有一次，他臥底為一個名為馬爾科的罪犯的保鏢。

At that time, Clint already created his new **identity** "Hawkeye" and was working with his new mentor from the carnival Trick Shot to rob Marko's mansion. He shot Barney and before Barney could figure out who he was, he left.

當時，柯林已經創造了他的新身份「鷹眼」，並與他的新導師「捷射」一起搶劫馬爾科的豪宅。他槍殺哥哥巴尼，而在巴尼能分辨出他到底是誰時他離開了。

Barney turned down another cover mission, which made Egghead pissed off. Egghead **destroyed** his FBI team. Barney

巴尼拒絕另一個臥底任務，因而惹怒了理論家。理論家毀了他的FBI團隊。巴

went to the Avengers for help but ended up sacrificing himself, to stop Egghead's ray projector from harming others. At his **funeral**, Clint finally found out about his brother's double life, and the fact that his brother was fully **aware** of Clint's double life as well.

尼跑到復仇者那裡尋求幫助，但最後還是犧牲了自己，以防止理論家的射線投影傷害到其他人。在他的葬禮時，柯林終於知道了他哥哥的雙重生活，而事實上，他的哥哥也完全知道柯林的雙重生活。

卡漫精選字彙表

單字	詞性	中譯	單字	詞性	中譯
stint	*v.*	停止	approach	*v.*	著手處理
undercover	*n.*	臥底	exchange	*v.*	交換
bodyguard	*n.*	保鏢	destroy	*v.*	破壞
identity	*n.*	身分	funeral	*n.*	葬禮
betray	*v.*	背叛	aware	*adj.*	知道的
figure out	*v.*	弄清楚			

01 劃時代的傳奇

02 不朽的英雄神話

03 無堅不摧背後的英雄血淚

04 永存於人們心中的英雄霸主

MP3 96

From Death to Devil
從死亡變為魔鬼

Barney's body was kept in a stasis by Egghead. Years later Zemo **dug up** Barney's background and **revived** him and manipulated him to go against Hawkeye. Zemo then found Hawkeye's other mentor, Trick Shot. Trick Shot was **suffering** from cancer.

Zemo promised to **fund** Trick Shot's medical treatment if he taught Barney how to **wield** a bow. Trick Shot did so, but did not receive the fund he was promised. Before Trick Shot dies, Zemo dropped Trick Shot off to Hawkeye and left a message with a bow.

When Clint was investigating his mentor's death, Barney

理論家讓巴尼的血流停滯。幾年後澤莫挖出了巴尼的背景，使他甦醒過來，並操縱他與鷹眼作對。澤莫隨後發現鷹眼的其他導師，捷射。捷射身患癌症。

澤莫答應資助捷射的治療，條件是如果他教巴尼如何使用弓。捷射這樣做了，但沒有收到他承諾的資金。捷射在死之前，澤莫將他丟給鷹眼，並留了一只弓當作留言。

當柯林正在調查他的恩師之死時，巴

ambushed him and declared himself as the NEW TRICK SHOT. He captured Clint to Zemo. Zemo then arranged the brothers to fight to the death. Hawkeye was able to defeat Barney and capture him alive. The relationship between the brothers did not recover though. As the NEW TRICK SHOT, Barney was later on invited to become the incarnation of the Dark Avengers to replace Bullseye as the new Dark Hawkeye.

尼伏擊他並宣布自己為新的捷射。他捕捉到柯林並將他交給澤莫。澤莫之後安排兄弟決一死戰。鷹眼擊敗了巴尼並活捉了他。兄弟之間的關係，終究沒有恢復。作為新的捷射，巴尼後來就受邀成為黑暗復仇者的化身，以取代「靶眼」作為新的闇黑鷹眼。

卡漫精選字彙表

單字	詞性	中譯	單字	詞性	中譯
stasis	v.	停滯	wield	v.	使用
dig up	v.	挖出	ambush	v.	突襲
revive	v.	復活	declare	v.	宣布
suffer	v.	受苦	incarnation	n.	化身
fund	v.	提供資金			

01 劃時代的傳奇

02 不朽的英雄神話

03 無堅不摧背後的英雄血淚

04 永存於人們心中的英雄霸主

必考字彙大回顧

卡漫超給力字彙表

單字	中譯	詞性	反義字	反義字中譯
assistant	助理	*n.*		
distance	使遠離	*v.*	associate	使相關
condemn	譴責	*v.*	commend	表彰
ultimatum	最後通牒	*n.*		
disappointedly	失望地	*adv.*	contentedly	滿足地
stint	停止	*v.*		
undercover	臥底	*n.*	public	公開
bodyguard	保鏢	*n.*		
identity	身分	*n.*		
betray	背叛	*v.*	stand by	支持
figure out	弄清楚	*v.*	confuse	困惑
approach	著手處理	*v.*	avoid	避免
exchange	交換	*v.*	hold	保持
destroy	破壞	*v.*	conserve	養護
funeral	葬禮	*n.*		
aware	知道的	*adj.*	unaware	不知道的
stasis	停滯	*v.*	change	更改
dig up	挖出	*v.*	bury	埋葬
revive	復活	*v.*	kill	殺害
suffer	受苦	*v.*	abstain	避免
fund	提供資金	*v.*		

單字	中譯	詞性	反義字	反義字中譯
wield	使用	*v.*	**cease**	停止
ambush	突襲	*v.*		
declare	宣布	*v.*	**veto**	否決
incarnation	化身	*n.*		

01 劃時代的傳奇

02 不朽的英雄神話

03 無堅不摧背後的英雄血淚

04 永存於人們心中的英雄霸主

The Black Widow Program
黑寡婦計劃

Natasha Romanova was an orphan who was **trapped** in a burning building during an attack on Stalingrad by enemy forces. She was found and rescued by a Soviet soldier named Petrovitch Bezukhov, who later on became her dearest friend and father figure.

In 1941, she was almost **brainwashed** by the ninja clan "the Hand", but luckily was saved by Logan. She then was recruited to become part of the Black Widow Program which was a team of **elite** female agents.

At the program, all female agents were **biotechnologically** and **psycho-technologically enhanced.**

娜塔莎諾娃是個在被敵軍斯大林格勒的一次襲擊中,被困在正在燃燒中大樓的孤兒。她是被一位名為彼得羅維奇的蘇聯士兵所發現的。這個人後來成為了她最親密的朋友和父親。

1941年,她幾乎被忍者家族的「合手黨」給洗腦了,但幸運的被洛根所救。然後,她被招募進入黑寡婦計劃,一個精英女特工團隊。

在訓練中,所有的女特工的生物技術和心理技術皆被增

They all have unusual young look like they never aged, they are also resistant to diseases and heal at an above human rate. They were all **deployed** with false memories to **ensure** their loyalty.

強。她們都具有異於常人的年輕樣貌及年齡不會增長的技能。她們也可以抵抗疾病，並可以以快於人類的速度癒合。他們都用虛假記憶部署，以確保她們的忠誠度。

卡漫精選字彙表

單字	詞性	中譯	單字	詞性	中譯
widow	*n.*	寡婦	psyco-technologically	*adv.*	心理技術地
trap	*v.*	困住	enhance	*v.*	增強
brainwash	*v.*	洗腦	deploy	*v.*	部署
elite	*n.*	精英	ensure	*v.*	確保
biotechnologically	*adv.*	生物技術地			

01 劃時代的傳奇

02 不朽的英雄神話

03 無堅不摧背後的英雄血淚

04 永存於人們心中的英雄霸主

MP3 98

The Femme Fatale
蛇蠍美人

Natasha was trained to become a world class athlete, acrobat, and **aerialist** capable of **numerous maneuvers** and feats. Since she was **characterized** to be a **ballerina**, she also learned marvelous ballet skill as well. During her training days, she fell shortly in love with her instructor Winter Soldier. However, she was later on **arranged** to marry a champion test pilot, Alexi Shostakov. Natasha did end up falling in love with Shostakov, but the KGB **faked** Shostakov's death and made Natasha a real widow.

Natasha was described as a

娜塔莎被培養成為一名世界級的運動員、雜技演員和一個可以進行各種演習和功勳的高空達人。因為她的特點是一個芭蕾舞演員，她也學會了了不起的芭蕾舞技巧。在她接受訓練時，她便愛上了她的教練寒天戰士。不過，她後來被安排嫁給一個冠軍的試飛員，阿列克謝。娜塔莎最終是愛上了阿列克謝，但KGB偽造了阿列克謝的死，使得娜塔莎成為一位真正的寡婦。

娜塔莎被描述為

femme fatale. Her first mission was to assist Boris Turgenov in the **assassination** of Professor Anton Vanko for **defecting** from the Soviet Union. They **infiltrated** Stark Industries and manipulated information from American defense contractor Tony Strak. Fortunately, Iron Man showed up and **inevitably confronted** Natasha. Iron Man and the two went into battle. Vanko sacrificed himself to save Iron Man and killed Turgenov at the same time.

一個蛇蠍美人。她的第一個任務是幫助包里斯刺殺從蘇聯叛逃的安東萬科教授。他們滲透進史塔克產業，並操縱美國國防承包商托尼史塔克的信息。還好，鋼鐵人出現了，無可避免地面對娜塔莎。鋼鐵人與他們兩位開始互戰。萬科犧牲自己來拯救鋼鐵人，並在同一時間殺死了包里斯。

卡漫精選字彙表

單字	詞性	中譯	單字	詞性	中譯
aerialist	*n.*	高空特技員	fake	*adj.*	假的
numerous	*adj.*	眾多的	assassination	*n.*	暗殺
maneuver	*n.*	演習	defect	*v.*	缺陷
characterize	*v.*	描繪為	infiltrate	*v.*	浸潤
ballerina	*n.*	芭蕾舞演員	inevitably	*adj.*	必然的
arrange	*v.*	安排	confront	*v.*	面對

From Bad to Good
從壞變好

Later on, Natasha met Hawkeye and manipulated him to go against Iron Man. However, during a fight in between Hawkeye and Iron Man, Black Widow was badly injured. In order to save her, Hawkeye **retreated** to get her to safety. Falling in love with Hawkeye, Natasha's loyalty to her country was **weakened**. Even so, she still left Hawkeye. She once again was brainwashed and battled the Avengers. Although, she eventually received the help from Hawkeye, she broke free from her **psychological** condition.

Later on, she joined the S.H.I.E.L.D. and started the

後來，娜塔莎遇到鷹眼並開始操縱他，使他與鋼鐵人作對。然而，在鷹眼和鋼鐵人之間的戰鬥中，黑寡婦受了重傷。為了她的安全，鷹眼撤退，並帶她到安全的地方。在她愛上鷹眼的同時，娜塔莎對她國家的忠誠度也逐漸減弱。即便如此，她還是離開了鷹眼。她再次被洗腦並且與復仇者作戰。雖然她最終得到來自鷹眼的幫助，突破了她的心理狀態。

後來，她加入了S.H.I.E.L.D.並啟動

international missions. She was then romantically involved with Matt Murdock who later on became the Daredevil in San Francisco. They operated as independent superheroes. After they broke up, Natasha then moved to Los Angeles and formed a new super team known as The Champions, but group didn't last long.

了國際任務。然後，她與之後變身為夜行俠的馬特默多克在一起。他們住在舊金山。並作為獨立的超級英雄。他們分手後，娜塔莎則搬到了洛杉磯，並組成了一個「成功者」的球隊。但這個集團並沒有持續多久。

卡漫精選字彙表

單字	詞性	中譯	單字	詞性	中譯
retreat	*v.*	撤退	psycological	*adj.*	心理學的
weaken	*v.*	使……變弱			

必考字彙大回顧

卡漫超給力字彙表

單字	中譯	詞性	反義字	反義字中譯
widow	寡婦	*n.*		
trap	困住	*v.*	release	放出
brainwash	洗腦	*v.*	remain	維持
elite	精英	*n.*	ordinary	普通
biotechnologically	生物技術地	*adv.*		
psyco-technologically	心理技術地	*adv.*		
enhance	增強	*v.*	diminish	減少
deploy	部署	*v.*		
ensure	確保	*v.*	endanger	危害
femme fatale	蛇蠍美人	*n.*		
aerialist	高空特技員	*n.*		
numerous	眾多的	*adj.*	few	少數的
maneuver	演習	*n.*		
characterize	描繪為	*v.*	mix up	混合
ballerina	芭蕾舞演員	*n.*		
arrange	安排	*v.*	disarrange	打亂
fake	假的	*adj.*	genuine	真的
assassination	暗殺	*n.*		
defect	缺陷	*v.*		
infiltrate	浸潤	*v.*		
inevitably	必然的	*adj.*		

單字	中譯	詞性	反義字	反義字中譯
confront	面對	*v.*	avoid	避免
retreat	撤退	*v.*	continue	繼續
weaken	使……變弱	*v.*	strengthen	加強
psycological	心理學的	*adj.*		

The Supreme Pilot
最好的機長

Born in Moscow, Alexei Shastakov was known for being the Black Widow Natasha Romanova's husband. Both of them were agents of the Soviets.

During World War II, Alexei shot down a large number of Luftwaffe fighter planes in **aerial** battles and was **credited** for helping the Soviet Air Force win air **supremacy** over the skies of Stalingrad and Kursk. Alexei was considered one of the most **acclaimed** pilots of the Soviet Union. He was also the first pilot who test flew the Mig 15. Later on, he fought against the U.S Air Force during the Korean War. He was then assigned to marry the famous ballerina Natasha Romanova.

出生於莫斯科，阿列克謝是黑寡婦娜塔莎諾娃的丈夫。他們兩個都是蘇聯的特勤。

二戰期間，阿列克謝擊落了大量的空軍戰機，並幫助蘇聯空軍贏得控制斯大林格勒和庫爾斯克天空的權利。阿列克謝可以説是蘇聯最知名的飛行員之一。他還在朝鮮戰爭期間進行米格15的測試。後來，他在韓戰期間與美軍對戰，爾後，被任命與著名的芭蕾舞演員娜塔莎羅曼諾娃結婚。

卡漫精選字彙表

單字	詞性	中譯	單字	詞性	中譯
aerial	*adj.*	航空的	supremacy	*n.*	主權
credit	*n.*	信用	acclaim	*v.*	歡呼

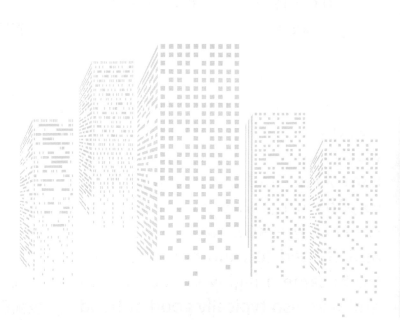

01 劃時代的傳奇

02 不朽的英雄神話

03 無堅不摧背後的英雄血淚

04 永存於人們心中的英雄霸主

MP3 101

The Secret Creation of the Red Guardian
紅衛士的秘密創作

As the Cold War **flared** up, the Soviet government realized that the country needed an **equivalent** to Captain America. Alexi became the chosen one. During a mission away from home, Alexi was **informed** of the new plans and was told not to have any contact with any of his past friends and **acquaintances**.

He was not allowed to contact his wife either. **Meanwhile**, Natasha was informed by a Soviet official that Alexi had been killed in an explosion of an **experimental** rocket. The KGB faked his death and started to train him in secret. He became a highly skilled athlete and was also typically good at hand

隨著冷戰爆發後，蘇聯政府意識到該國需要一個相當於美國隊長的人。阿列克謝成了不二人選。在一次離家的任務之中，阿列克謝得知這一新的計劃。他同時被告知不要跟任何過去的朋友和熟人做任何接觸。

他也不能聯繫他的妻子。同時，娜塔莎也被蘇聯政府通知說阿列克謝已經在實驗火箭爆炸時被殺害。KGB偽造了他的死亡，並開始他的秘密訓練。他成了一名技術高超的運動員，

to hand combat.

The KGB even made him his signature weapon, the disc. The disc had a yellow hammer and **sickle** symbol on it to represent the Soviet Union. It is oftentimes attached to his belt and can automatically return after being thrown using **magnetic** forces. He also started to wear his new costume, and changed his name to the "Red Guardian."

也善於肉搏戰。

KGB甚至給了他他的知名武器，光盤。光盤上有一個黃色錘子和鐮刀的象徵，代表了蘇聯。它往往把光盤放在腰帶上，且可以使用磁力讓被拋出後的光盤自動返回。他也開始穿他的新服裝，並改名為「紅衛士」。

卡漫精選字彙表

單字	詞性	中譯	單字	詞性	中譯
flare	*v.*	閃耀	meanwhile	*adv.*	與此同時
equivalent	*adj.*	相等的	experimental	*adj.*	實驗的
inform	*v.*	通知	sickle	*n.*	鐮刀
acquaintance	*n.*	相識	magnetic	*adj.*	有磁性的

01 劃時代的傳奇

02 不朽的英雄神話

03 無堅不摧背後的英雄血淚

04 永存於人們心中的英雄霸主

Remain Loyal to His Government
仍然忠於他的政府

Unlike the Black Widow who became **disillusioned** with the KGB, the Red Guardian remains loyal to his government. He even became more **ruthless** and **vindictive**. One time, he was sent to China to help protect a Communist Chinese secret weapon located at a secret military base at an unknown location.

He ended up **encountering** the Black Widow and Captain America. The Black Widow noticed something was familiar but couldn't tell what until the Red Guardian revealed his true identity to her. He was then shot and **mortally** wounded.

He then was buried under

不像黑寡婦使KGB幻滅，紅衛士仍然忠於他的政府。他甚至變得更加無情和鬥氣。有一次，他被派往中國，以幫助保護中國共產黨一個位於秘密軍事基地處於未揭露位置的神秘武器。

最後他遇到了黑寡婦和美國隊長。黑寡婦覺得很熟悉卻說不出什麼，直到紅衛士暴露了他的真實身份讓她知道。然後，他中槍，受了致命傷。

爾後淹沒在熔岩

molten lava. Years later, he was revealed to be alive and had risen very high in power within Bulgaria and Ronin. He started his mission to catch his former wife and **try** her for the crimes.

底下。多年以後，有人透露他還活著，並活躍在保加利亞和羅寧。他的能力有有著大大的進步。他開始了他的使命追捕他的前妻，並審判她的罪行。

卡漫精選字彙表

單字	詞性	中譯	單字	詞性	中譯
disillusion	*n.*	醒悟	encounter	*v.*	遭遇
ruthless	*adj.*	無情的	mortally	*adv.*	致命地
vindictive	*adj.*	有復仇心的	try	*v.*	審判

01 劃時代的傳奇

02 不朽的英雄神話

03 無堅不摧背後的英雄血淚

04 永存於人們心中的英雄霸主

卡漫超給力字彙表

單字	中譯	詞性	反義字	反義字中譯
aerial	航空的	*adj.*	ground	地面的
credit	信用	*n.*	discredit	懷疑
supremacy	主權	*n.*	inferiority	次等
acclaim	歡呼	*v.*	criticize	批評
flare	閃耀	*v.*		
equivalent	相等的	*adj.*	different	不同的
inform	通知	*v.*	keep in the dark	保持在黑暗中
acquaintance	相識	*n.*	stranger	陌生人
meanwhile	與此同時	*adv.*		
experimental	實驗的	*adj.*		
sickle	鐮刀	*n.*		
magnetic	有磁性的	*adj.*		
disillusion	醒悟	*n.*	inspire	啟發
ruthless	無情的	*adj.*	merciful	仁慈的
vindictive	有復仇新的	*adj.*	kind	友善的
encounter	遭遇	*v.*	doudge	躲閃
mortally	致命地	*adv.*	mildly	輕度地
try	審判	*v.*		

MP3 103

The Split Personality Caused by the Childhood Tragedy
童年的悲劇所造成的人格分裂

It's hard for most people to imagine being born in a family with **abusive** parents. Unfortunately, Robert Bruce Banner was one of those kids. The son of an alcoholic, Banner was hated by his **atomic physicist** father who worked on producing clean **nuclear** power as an energy source.

Dr. Brian Banner believed that his son's intelligence came from the **exposure** to the nuclear power. He believed that his son had been mutated and was indeed a monster. Banner's mother tried to stop Brian but ended up getting murdered. Brian was then sent to a

大多數人都難以想像出生在有會虐待孩子的父母的家庭。不幸的是,羅伯特‧布魯斯‧班寧就是那些孩子之一。一個酒鬼的兒子,班寧被父親所憎恨,他父親是個酒鬼,也是一位核能原子物理學家,致力生產環保核能。

布萊恩‧班寧博士相信他兒子的聰穎是從曝光到核電所得到的。他認為,他的兒子已經突變並確實是一個怪物。班寧的母親試圖阻止布萊恩,但最終被殺害。

psychiatric institute.

Due to the childhood **tragedy**, Banner developed a **split** personality. He found it hard to develop friendships and often being picked on while he was in school. One day, he built and planted a bomb in his school which caused the explosion. Of course he was not only expelled but also caught the military's attention. Banner was later hired by the military after he earned a **doctorate** in nuclear physics.

然後布萊恩就被被送往精神病研究所。

由於童年的悲劇，班寧產生了人格的分裂。他發現他很難發展友誼，他在學校時，經常被欺負。有一天他在學校製作並埋了一個炸彈，引發爆炸。他當然被開除了，但同時也引起了軍方的重視。班寧後來在獲得核物理學博士後，被軍方聘請。

卡漫精選字彙表

單字	詞性	中譯	單字	詞性	中譯
split	v.	分裂	nuclear	adj.	原子核的
tragedy	n.	悲劇	exposure	n.	暴露
abusive	adj.	虐待的	psychiatric	adj.	精神病的
atomic	adj.	原子的	doctorate	n.	博士學位
physicist	n.	物理學家			

MP3 104

The Birth of the Hulk
浩克的誕生

An ignorant teenager wandered onto the testing field, while he was supervising the trial of an experimental gamma bomb he designed. To save him, Bruce was struck by bomb blast, causing some strange transformation in his body.

正當他在指揮一個他設計的伽瑪炸彈的實驗時，一個無知的少年遊蕩到測試領域。為了救他，布魯斯被炸彈所擊中，導致了身體有了奇怪的轉變。

At first, he will transform into a **brutish** gray Hulk only at sunset and **revert** to human form at **dawn**. Then, he would change into the **childlike** green Hulk when he gets **intensely** excited. Since the transformation, the Hulk also gained the **unlimited** strength. He was able to take Superman and Thor with his hands tied behind his back.

起初，他會變成一個粗野的灰色巨人，只在日落食變身，在黎明時恢復人形。然後，當他強烈興奮時，他會改變成綠色，像孩子的浩克。自轉型以來，浩克也獲得了無限的力量。即使他的雙手被反綁在背後，他還是能夠擊敗超人和雷

神。

He can also create a large **thunderclap**-type **concussive** force to hurt enemies, to put out fire or **deafen** people. His legs are **augmented** so much that he can travel miles in a single jump. His skin allows protection from bullets, grenades and rockets. He also has the quickest healing factor and the ability to resist mind control.

他也可以創建一個大霹靂式的震盪來傷害敵人，滅火或使人變聾。他的腿力大增，一個跳躍即可行走好幾英里。他的皮膚可以防子彈、手榴彈和火箭。他還擁有最快的癒合因子和不被精神控制的能力。

01 劃時代的傳奇

02 不朽的英雄神話

03 無堅不摧背後的英雄血淚

04 永存於人們心中的英雄霸主

卡漫精選字彙表

單字	詞性	中譯	單字	詞性	中譯
supervise	*v.*	監督	childlike	*adj.*	孩子似的
trial	*n.*	試驗	intensely	*adv.*	激烈地
ignorant	*adj.*	愚昧的	unlimited	*adj.*	無限的
wander	*v.*	漫步	thunderclap	*n.*	霹靂
brutish	*adj.*	野蠻的	concussive	*adj.*	震盪的
revert	*v.*	還原	deafen	*v.*	使變聾
dawn	*n.*	黎明	augment	*v.*	增加

Friends and Foes
朋友和敵人

Since his transformation, he was **hunted** by the military forces **continually**, but later he helped the government to destroy the alien Metal Master and received a presidential **pardon**. After that, he teamed up with many superheroes who thought he wasn't all bad.

由於他的轉變，他不斷地被軍隊捕殺，直到後來，他幫助政府消滅外星金屬隊長，並獲得總統特赦。之後，他與許多認為他也不完全是壞人的超級英雄們聯手。

Starting from Spider-Man and Iron Fist to the Avengers like the Thing and Wolverine, they all partnered with Hulk on several **occasions**. They fought against him too since the Hulk has the split personality which he couldn't control easily.

從蜘蛛人開始，到鐵拳、復仇者的金剛狼和石頭人等，他們都與浩克合作多次。他們與他也對立過，因為浩克有分裂的人格，他不能輕易控制。

Because of the **disadvantage**, the Hulk could easily be

因為這個缺點，浩克很容易被操縱，

manipulated and used by the villains in short time to harm people too. Gamma-powered psychiatrist Leonard "Doc" Samson once captured the Hulk and successfully separated Banner and the Hulk.

This action made the Hulk the ultimate monster who only has the strength but doesn't have the intelligence to control his actions. Realizing the only solution to rein in the Hulk is to **merge** with the monster again, Banner did so.

並被壞人短時間的利用來傷害人類。伽瑪力學的心理醫生倫納德「醫師」山森有一次捕獲浩克,並成功的分離了班寧和浩克。

這個舉動使得浩克成為了一個只有蠻力但沒有足夠的智慧來控制自己行動的怪物。了解到惟有再與浩克結合才能解決這個問題,班寧就這麼做了。

卡漫精選字彙表

單字	詞性	中譯	單字	詞性	中譯
hunt	*v.*	追捕	occasion	*n.*	場合
continually	*adv.*	不斷地	disadvantage	*n.*	壞處
pardon	*n.*	赦免	merge	*v.*	合併

必考字彙大回顧

卡漫超給力字彙表

單字	中譯	詞性	反義字	反義字中譯
split	分裂	*v.*	combine	結合
tragedy	悲劇	*n.*	blessing	幸福的事
abusive	虐待的	*adj.*	kind	和藹的
atomic	原子的	*adj.*		
physicist	物理學家	*n.*		
nuclear	原子核的	*adj.*		
exposure	暴露	*n.*	hiding	隱藏
psychiatric	精神病的	*adj.*		
doctorate	博士學位	*n.*		
supervise	監督	*v.*	follow	跟隨
trial	試驗	*n.*		
ignorant	愚昧的	*adj.*	educated	博學的
wander	漫步	*v.*	run	跑
brutish	野蠻的	*adj.*	humane	人道的
revert	還原	*v.*		
dawn	黎明	*n.*	sunset	日落
childlike	孩子似的	*adj.*		
intensely	激烈地	*adv.*	mildly	輕度地
unlimited	無限的	*adj.*	limited	有限的
thunderclap	霹靂	*n.*		
concussive	震盪的	*adj.*		
deafen	使變聾	*v.*		

單字	中譯	詞性	反義字	反義字中譯
augment	增加	*v.*	**diminish**	減少
hunt	追捕	*v.*	**let go**	放開
continually	不斷地	*adv.*	**intermittently**	間歇性地
pardon	赦免	*n.*	**conviction**	定罪
occasion	場合	*n.*		
disadvantage	壞處	*n.*	**advantage**	優點
merge	合併	*v.*	**separate**	分離

MP3 106

Exposed to the Gamma Radiation
暴露於伽瑪射線

Samuel Sterns had a not so happy childhood. He eventually dropped out of high school.

塞繆‧史塔恩有著不那麼幸福的童年。他最終在高中輟學。

One day, when Samuel was moving a **cylinder** of radioactive waste, he was caught in an unexpected explosion. Just like the Hulk, he was exposed to the Gamma radiation. He was soon sent to the ER, but while he was **recovering** in the hospital, he started to have an **insatiable thirst** for knowledge.

有一天,當塞繆在移動放射性廢物缸時,他陷入了一個意想不到的爆炸。就像浩克,他接觸到伽瑪輻射。他很快被送到急診室,但是當他在醫院恢復時,他開始對知識有著貪得無厭的渴求。

He started to read through everything he could lay his hands on. Weeks later, his skin turned green and his skull **expanded** upwards. He transformed into the

他開始閱讀一切他拿得到的東西。幾個星期後,他的皮膚變成綠色,他的頭骨向上擴展。他變成超

hyper-intelligent Leader. His intelligence allows him to **predict** possibilities and the **outcomes** are normally correct. His **assumptions** are almost correct and he is able to recall any events because of his perfect memory. He also has the ability to control other people's minds. Because of his **miserable** childhood, he decided to use intelligence to bring him the power and the **prestigious** life which he didn't have before.

級智能領導者。他的智慧讓他能預測可能性，而且結果通常是正確的。他的假設也通常是正確的，他能夠完美的記憶任何事件。他也有能力控制別人的心靈。由於他苦難的童年，他決定用智慧，帶給他力量和他以前沒有信譽的生活。

卡漫精選字彙表

單字	詞性	中譯	單字	詞性	中譯
cylinder	*n.*	汽缸	predict	*v.*	預測
recover	*v.*	恢復	outcome	*n.*	結果
insatiable	*adj.*	貪心的	assumption	*n.*	假設
thirst	*n.*	渴望	miserable	*adj.*	慘痛的
expand	*v.*	擴大	prestigious	*adj.*	享譽盛名的
hyper	*adj.*	亢奮的			

The Non-Stop Feud
不停的宿怨

He then organized a spy ring to steal scientific secrets. He became the most **consistent** and dangerous **creature** who desires to take over the United States and eventually conquer the world. Both transformed by the Gamma radiation, the Leader first thought that the Hulk would join his spy ring without a doubt.

However, things went differently. The Hulk became an **impediment** to his plan. Instead of fighting against the superhero teams, the Hulk actually group up with them to **combat** with the Leader. Desperate to study his foe, the Leader first sent the Chameleon and **synthetic** Humanoids to capture the Hulk.

爾後，他組織了一個間諜網，專偷科學秘密。他成為了最一貫的和危險的生物，夢想要接手美國並最終統治世界。由於兩個都是被伽瑪射線所改變，首腦毫無疑問的原本想要叫浩克加入他的間諜網。

然而，事情進展並不相同。浩克成為了阻礙他計劃的人。與其與超級英雄們對戰，浩克與他們團結一同對抗首腦。渴望了解他的敵人，首腦首先送了變色龍和合成人去捕捉浩克。

This action stated the non-stop **feud** between the two of them. The desire to conquer the world led the Leader to construct an army of powerful **obedient** plastic robots called Humanoids and a space station named Omnivac. He also recruited a whole bunch of villains such as Rhino, Abomination and Half-Life. He sometimes partnered with General "Thunderbolt" Ross and MODOK.

這個動作開始了他們兩個人之間不停的爭執。想要統治世界的慾望導致首腦來構建強大的塑料機器人，被稱為類人生物的軍隊和一個名為Omnivac的航空站。他還找來一大堆壞人，如犀牛，憎惡和半條命。他有時也會與大將軍「迅雷」羅斯和MODOK合作。

卡漫精選字彙表

單字	詞性	中譯	單字	詞性	中譯
consistent	*adj.*	一貫的	combat	*v.*	戰鬥
creature	*n.*	生物	feud	*n.*	世仇
impediment	*n.*	障礙	obedient	*adj.*	順從的

MP3 108

The New Society
新社會

One day, the Leader's mutation **destabilized**, and he reverted back to the **ordinary** Samuel Sterns. In order to regain his **heightened** intellect, he **drained** gamma radiation from Rick Jones who was also suffering from the gamma radiation transformation.

The Leader gained his power back. He later on created an **isolated** community hidden beneath the Columbia ice-fields of Alberta, Canada and named it Freehold. It was a place filled with people who are dying from radiation poisoning.

The Leader told the people there that Freehold would become

有一天，首腦的突變動搖了，他恢復到普通的塞繆・史塔恩。為了奪回自己的高智力，他喝乾了也為改造而痛苦的瑞克・瓊斯身上的伽瑪射線。

首腦重新獲得了他的力量。他後來在加拿大阿爾伯塔省的哥倫比亞冰下創造了一個孤立的社區，稱為永久業權。這個地方充滿了因為輻射中毒而快要死亡的人類。

首腦告訴那裡的人說，永久業權將成

the new society.

However, in reality, he was using the radiation victims for experiments. The Leader was once killed in a battle with the Hulk; however, his mind survived. His mind had **evolved** beyond the need for a body.

為新的社會。

然而，在現實中，他使用了輻射受害者進行實驗。首腦在與浩克的一場戰鬥時一度被殺害。然而，他的腦活了下來。後來他的腦已經演變成不需要身體也可以運作。

卡漫精選字彙表

單字	詞性	中譯	單字	詞性	中譯
destabilize	*v.*	不穩定	drain	*v.*	飲乾
ordinary	*adj.*	普通的	isolate	*v.*	隔離
heighten	*v.*	增加	evolve	*v.*	發展

01 劃時代的傳奇

02 不朽的英雄神話

03 無堅不摧背後的英雄血淚

04 永存於人們心中的英雄霸主

必考字彙大回顧

卡漫超給力字彙表

單字	中譯	詞性	反義字	反義字中譯
laborer	勞動者	n.		
facility	設施	n.		
brilliant	優秀的	adj.	dull	愚蠢的
talk down	駁倒			
cylinder	汽缸	n.		
recover	恢復	v.	damage	損傷
insatiable	貪心的	adj.	fulfilled	滿足的
thirst	渴望	n.		
expand	擴大	v.	compress	壓縮
hyper	亢奮的	adj.	calm	冷靜的
predict	預測	v.		
outcome	結果	n.	cause	原因
assumption	假設	n.	reality	現實
miserable	慘痛的	adj.	happy	快樂的
prestigious	享譽盛名的	adj		
consistent	一貫的	adj.	contradictory	矛盾的
creature	生物	n.		
impediment	障礙	n.	advantage	優點
combat	戰鬥	v.	support	支持
feud	世仇	n.	friendship	友誼
obedient	順從的	adj.	disobedient	忤逆的

單字	中譯	詞性	反義字	反義字中譯
destabilize	不穩定	*v.*	**stabilize**	使穩固
ordinary	普通的	*adj.*	**extraordinary**	非凡的
heighten	增加	*v.*	**decrease**	減少
drain	飲乾	*v.*	**replenish**	補充
isolate	隔離	*v.*	**include**	包括
evolve	發展	*v.*	**regress**	回歸

01 劃時代的傳奇

02 不朽的英雄神話

03 無堅不摧背後的英雄血淚

04 永存於人們心中的英雄霸主

Leader 051

首選必考 4000 單：「巧取」學測英文 15 級分+指考英文頂標（附 MP3）

作　　　者	洪婉婷
發 行 人	周瑞德
執行總監	齊心瑀
企劃編輯	陳韋佑
校　　對	編輯部
封面構成	高鍾琪

內頁構成	菩薩蠻數位文化有限公司
印　　製	大亞彩色印刷製版股份有限公司
初　　版	2016 年 10 月
定　　價	新台幣 380 元
出　　版	力得文化
電　　話	(02) 2351-2007
傳　　真	(02) 2351-0887
地　　址	100 台北市中正區福州街 1 號 10 樓之 2
E - m a i l	best.books.service@gmail.com
網　　址	www.bestbookstw.com

港澳地區總經銷	泛華發行代理有限公司
地　　　　址	香港新界將軍澳工業邨駿昌街 7 號 2 樓
電　　　　話	(852) 2798-2323
傳　　　　真	(852) 2796-5471

國家圖書館出版品預行編目資料

首選必考 4000 單：「巧取」學測英文 15
級分+指考英文頂標 / 洪婉婷著. -- 初
版. -- 臺北市：力得文化, 2016.10 面；
公 分 . -- (Leader ； 51)ISBN
978-986-93664-0-3 (平裝附光碟片)1.英
語教學 2.詞彙 3.中等教育

524.38　　　　　　　　105017162